# Let Us C Solutions

*19th Edition*

AF808687

**Yashavant Kanetkar**

www.bpbonline.com

**NINETEENTH REVISED & UPDATED EDITION 2023**
FIRST EDITION 2007

**Copyright © BPB Publications, India**

**© Let Us C is a registered trademark of BPB Publications, New Delhi under registration No. 1135514**

**ISBN: 978-93-5551-282-6**

All Rights Reserved. No part of this publication can be stored in a retrieval system or reproduced in any form or by any means without the prior written permission of the publishers.

## LIMITS OF LIABILITY AND DISCLAIMER OF WARRANTY

The Author and Publisher of this book have tried their best to ensure that the programmes, procedures and functions described in the book are correct. However, the author and the publishers make no warranty of any kind, expressed or implied, with regard to these programmes or the documentation contained in the book. The author and publisher shall not be liable in any event of any damages, incidental or consequential, in connection with, or arising out of the furnishing, performance or use of these programmes, procedures and functions. Product name mentioned are used for identification purposes only and may be trademarks of their respective companies.

All trademarks referred to in the book are acknowledged as properties of their respective owners.

To View Complete
BPB Publications Catalogue
Scan the QR Code:

www.bpbonline.com

*Dedicated to*
*Nalinee and Prabhakar Kanetkar*

## About the Author

Through his books and online Quest Video Courses on C, C++, Data Structures, VC++, .NET, Embedded Systems, etc. Yashavant Kanetkar has created, molded and groomed lacs of IT careers in the last two and half decades. Yashavant's books and online courses have made a significant contribution in creating top-notch IT manpower in India and abroad.

Yashavant's books are globally recognized and millions of students / professionals have benefitted from them. His books have been translated into Hindi, Gujarati, Japanese, Korean and Chinese languages. Many of his books are published in India, USA, Japan, Singapore, Korea and China.

Yashavant is a much sought-after speaker in the IT field and has conducted seminars/workshops at TedEx, IITs, NITs, IIITs and global software companies.

Yashavant has been honored with the prestigious "Distinguished Alumnus Award" by IIT Kanpur for his entrepreneurial, professional and academic excellence. This award was given to top 50 alumni of IIT Kanpur who have made significant contribution towards their profession and betterment of society in the last 50 years.

In recognition of his immense contribution to IT education in India, he has been awarded the "Best .NET Technical Contributor" and "Most Valuable Professional" awards by Microsoft for 5 successive years. Yashavant holds a BE from VJTI Mumbai and M. Tech. from IIT Kanpur. His current affiliations include being a Director of KICIT Pvt. Ltd. and an Adjunct Faculty at IIIT, Bangalore. He can be reached at kanetkar@kicit.com or through http://www.ykanetkar.com.

# Contents

# Introduction

The first requests for a book like 'Let Us C Solutions' started coming when the third edition of Let Us C was released. I answered them by writing this book. Since then, I have met so many readers who said that every new edition of Let Us C should be accompanied with two books—a new edition of 'Let Us C Solutions' and a new edition of 'Let Us C Workbook'. I decided to accede to this request and from fifth edition onwards started releasing all these three books simultaneously.

The success of last 18 editions of this book has validated my belief that if you have a book which lets a reader cross-check the solutions/programs that he creates, then it boosts his confidence and improves the overall language learning process.

Through all the editions of this book one person who never got tired of helping me was Manish Jain of BPB. No matter what request I made, he always acceded to it.

Amol Tambat, Ajay Daga, Prachi Garaye, Amit Mendhe, Vikrant Sahoo, Shoeb Parvez, Monali Nikhare and Devshree Satpute were instrumental in checking all the solutions of several editions of this book. Many thanks to all of them! I have reorganized and rationalized exercises of Let Us C $19^{th}$ edition. The solutions to all these exercises have been included in this edition of Let Us C Solutions.

# CHAPTER
# ZERO

# Before We Begin

To understand C language and gain confidence in working with it you would be required to type programs in this book and then instruct the machine to execute them. To type any program, you need another program called Editor. Once the program has been typed it needs to be converted to machine language (0s and 1s) before the machine can execute it. To carry out this conversion we need another program called Compiler. Compiler vendors provide an Integrated Development Environment (IDE) which consists of an Editor as well as the Compiler. These IDEs and its online alternatives are discussed in this appendix.

## IDEs

There are several IDEs available, each targeted towards different processor and operating system combinations. Given below is a brief description of the popular IDEs along with the links from where they can be downloaded.

### Turbo C/C++ under Windows

If you wish to use Turbo C/C++ it is available at

https://www.developerinsider.in/download-turbo-c-for-windows-7-8-8-1-and-windows-10-32-64-bit-full-screen/

It is very easy to install and it works for Windows 7, 8, 8.1 and Windows 10 (32/64 bit) with full/window screen mode.

### NetBeans under Windows

NetBeans is not a compiler. It is merely an IDE. Its Windows version can be downloaded from http://www.netbeans.org

For developing C programs using NetBeans under Windows, you would also have to install Cygwin software. Cygwin comes with GCC compiler. It is available at

https://www.cygwin.com/

There is a nice tutorial available at the following link should you face any difficulty in setting up Cygwin and NetBeans:

https://www.wikihow.com/Run-C/C%2B%2B-Program-in-Netbeans-on-Windows

### NetBeans under Linux

If you propose to use NetBeans under Linux you won't need Cygwin as with most Linux installations (like say, Ubuntu) GCC compiler comes preinstalled. So, you need to just download and install NetBeans for Linux environment.

### Visual Studio under Windows

If you wish to use Visual Studio Community it is available at

https://www.visualstudio.com/vs/express/

You are free to use any of the IDEs mentioned above for compiling programs in this book. If you wish to know my personal choice, I would prefer NetBeans + Cygwin or Visual Studio Community Edition. All the IDEs are easy to use and are available free of cost.

## Online Compilers

With ubiquitous availability of Internet, if you wish, you can completely avoid installation of IDE on your machine. Using a browser, you can connect to any of the following to type, compile and execute your programs:

https://www.onlinegdb.com/
https://www.tutorialspoint.com/compile_c_online.php

The limitation of using online compilers is that you need a steady Internet connection while you are using them. Most of these compilers compile our program using the gcc compiler.

# Compilation and Execution Steps in IDE

The compilation and execution process with each of the IDEs mentioned in the previous section are a bit different. So, for your benefit I am giving below these steps for each IDE.

## Compilation and Execution using Turbo C++

Carry out the following steps to compile and execute programs using Turbo C++:

(a) Start NetBeans from Start | All Programs | Turbo C++.

(b) Click 'Start Turbo C++' from the dialog that appears.

(c) Select File | New from menu.

(d) Type the program.

(e) Save the program using F2 under a proper name (say Program1.c).

(f) Use Ctrl + F9 to compile and execute the program.

(g) Use Alt + F5 to view the output.

## Compilation and Execution using NetBeans

Carry out the following steps to compile and execute programs using NetBeans:

(a) Start NetBeans from Start | All Programs | NetBeans.

(b) Select File | New Project... from the File menu. Select Project Category as C/C++ and Project Type as C/C++ Application from the dialog that pops up. Click Next button.

(c) Type a suitable project name (say Program1) in Project Name Textbox. Click Finish.

(d) Type the program.

(e) Save the program using Ctrl + S.

(f) Use F6 to compile and execute the program.

## Compilation and Execution using Visual Studio Community

Carry out the following steps to compile and execute programs using Visual Studio Community:

(a) Start Visual Studio Community from Start | All Programs | Microsoft Visual C++ Community.

(b) Select File | New Project... from the File menu. Select Project Type as C++ Console Application. Type a suitable project name (say Program1) in Project name Textbox. Choose suitable location where you wish to create the project folder. Click Create.

(c) Type the program.

(d) Save the program using Ctrl + S.

(e) Use Ctrl + F5 to compile and execute the program.

### Compilation and Execution at Linux Command-line

C programs can be compiled and executed even at command-line, i.e., without using any IDE. Many programmers prefer this mode. In such cases we need to use an editor like Vim to type the program and the GCC compiler to compile it. In such as case you need to follow the following steps to compile and execute your program.

(a) Type the program and save it under a suitable name, 'hello.c'.

(b) At the command prompt switch to the directory containing 'hello.c' using the **cd** command.

(c) Compile the program using GCC compiler as shown below.

```
$ gcc hello.c
```

(d) On successful compilation, GCC produces a file named 'a.out'. This file contains the machine language code of the program which can now be executed.

(e) Execute the program using the following command:

```
$ ./a.out
```

## Compilation and Execution Using Online Compilers

While using the online compilers you have to remember to choose the language (C in our case) from the dropdown. Next, we have to type our program and click the Run/Execute button. When we do so our typed program is sent to the web server where it is compiled and executed. The output created on execution is then sent back and displayed in the browser. If any errors are found in the program during compilation they are also relayed back and displayed in the browser.

In the past online compilers had a limitation that you could run only single file programs using them. This has been overcome now. For example, in www.onlinegdb.com you can create a multi-file project easily. For this you have to first login using your google account and then click on the menu item 'Create New Project' from the left column in the browser window. This will create a skeleton file by the name 'main.c'. In this file you can type **main( )**. Then either use Ctrl M or by clicking the 'New File' icon in the top toolbar you can add a new file with a suitable name. We can add multiple files in this manner. Then run the project as usual by clicking on the 'Run' button.

Onlinegdb.com also has provisions to supply command-line arguments, debug a program using the debugger, create folders and store multiple files in it. From the point of view of security online compilers is not a preferred choice for serious software development in C. Nevertheless, a good option with zero installation and configuration headaches when you are learning C.

# CHAPTER ONE

# Getting Started

**[A]** Which of the following are invalid C constants and why?

| | |
|---|---|
| ’3.15’ | Invalid. A character constant can contain only 1 character |
| 35,550 | Invalid. An integer constant cannot contain a comma |
| 3.25e2 | Valid |
| 2e-3 | Valid |
| ’eLearning’ | Invalid. A character constant can contain only 1 character |
| "show" | Invalid. A character constant can contain only 1 character |
| ’Quest’ | Invalid. A character constant can contain only 1 character |
| $2^3$ | Invalid. Number cannot be expressed in this form |
| 4 6 5 2 | Invalid. There cannot be a space within a constant |

**[B]** Which of the following are invalid variable names and why?

| | |
|---|---|
| B’day | Invalid. A ‘’’ is not allowed in variable name |
| int | Invalid. Keyword cannot be used as a variable name |
| $hello | Invalid. Variable name must begin with an alphabet or underscore |
| #HASH | Invalid. Variable name must begin with an alphabet or underscore |
| dot. | Invalid. A ‘.’ is not allowed in variable name |

| | |
|---|---|
| number | Valid |
| totalArea | Valid |
| _main( ) | Valid |
| temp_in_Deg | Valid |
| total% | Invalid. A '%' is not allowed in variable name |
| 1st | Invalid. A variable name must start with an alphabet or an underscore |
| stack-queue | Invalid. We cannot use hyphen in variable name |
| variable name | Invalid. Variable name cannot contain spaces |
| %name% | Invalid. A variable name must start with an alphabet or an underscore |
| salary | Valid |

**[C]** State whether the following statements are True or False:

(a) C language has been developed by Dennis Ritchie.

Answer: True

(b) Operating systems like Windows, Unix, Linux and Android are written in C.

Answer: True

(c) C language programs can easily interact with hardware of a PC / Laptop.

Answer: True

(d) A real constant in C can be expressed in both Fractional and Exponential forms

Answer: True

(e) A character variable can at a time store only one character.

Answer: True

(f) The maximum value that an integer constant can have varies from one compiler to another.

Answer: True

(g) Usually, all C statements are entered in small case letters.

Answer: True

(h) Spaces may be inserted between two words in a C statement.

Answer: True

(i) Spaces cannot be present within a variable name.

Answer: True

(j) C programs are converted into machine language with the help of a program called Editor.

Answer: False

(k) Most development environments provide an Editor to type a C program and a Compiler to convert it into machine language.

Answer: True

(l) **int, char, float, real, integer, character, char, main, printf** and **scanf** are keywords.

Answer: False

**[D]** Match the following pairs:

| | |
|---|---|
| (a) \n | (4) Escape sequence |
| (b) 3.145 | (12) Real constant |
| (c) -6513 | (7) Integer constant |
| (d) 'D' | (3) Character constant |
| (e) 4.25e-3 | (11) Exponential form |
| (f) main( ) | (6) Function |
| (g) %f, %d, %c | (10) Format specifier |
| (h) ; | (2) Statement terminator |
| (i) Constant | (1) Literal |
| (j) Variable | (13) Identifier |
| (k) & | (8) Address of operator |
| (l) printf( ) | (9) Output function |
| (m) scanf( ) | (5) Input function |

**[E]** Point out the errors, if any, in the following programs:

(a)
```
int main( )
{
    int a ; float b ; int c ;
    a = 25 ; b = 3.24 ; c = a + b * b – 35 ;
```

```
}
```

No error. Multiple C statements can be written in a single line.

(b)
```
#include <stdio.h>
int main( )
{
    int a = 35 ; float b = 3.24 ;
    printf ( "%d %f %d", a, b + 1.5, 235 ) ;
}
```

No error. The list being printed in **printf( )** may contain variables, constants or expressions.

(c)
```
#include <stdio.h>
int main( )
{
    int a, b, c ;
    scanf ( "%d %d %d", a, b, c ) ;
}
```

Error. We should use & before each variable used in **scanf( )**.

(d)
```
#include <stdio.h>
int main( )
{
    int m1, m2, m3
    printf ( "Enter values of marks in 3 subjects: " )
    scanf ( "%d %d %d", &m1, &m2, &m3 )
    printf ( "You entered %d %d %d", m1, m2, m3 )
}
```

Error. Semicolon should be present at the end of type declaration, **printf( )** and **scanf( )** statements.

**[F]** Attempt the following questions:

(a) Temperature of a city in Fahrenheit degrees is input through the keyboard. Write a program to convert this temperature into Centigrade degrees.

*Program:*

```
/* Conversion of temperature from Fahrenheit to Centigrade */
# include <stdio.h>
int main( )
{
    float fr, cent ;
    printf ( "\nEnter the temperature (F): " ) ;
    scanf ( "%f", &fr ) ;
    cent = 5.0 / 9.0 * ( fr - 32 ) ;
    printf ( "Temperature in centigrade = %f\n", cent ) ;
    return 0 ;
}
```

(b) The length & breadth of a rectangle and radius of a circle are input through the keyboard. Write a program to calculate the area and perimeter of the rectangle, and the area and circumference of the circle.

*Program:*

```
/* Calculation of perimeter & area of rectangle and circle */
# include <stdio.h>
int main( )
{
    int l, b, r, area1, perimeter ;
    float area2, circum ;
    printf ( "\nEnter Length & Breadth of Rectangle: " ) ;
    scanf ( "%d %d", &l, &b ) ;
    area1 = l * b ; /* Area of a rectangle */
    perimeter = 2 * l + 2 * b ; /* Perimeter of a rectangle */
    printf ( "Area of Rectangle = %d\n", area1 ) ;
    printf ( "Perimeter of Rectangle = %d\n", perimeter) ;
    printf ( "\n\nEnter Radius of circle: " ) ;
    scanf ( "%d", &r ) ;
    area2 = 3.14 * r * r ; /* Area of Circle */
    circum = 2 * 3.14 * r ; /* Circumference of a circle */
    printf ( "Area of Circle = %f\n", area2 ) ;
    printf ( "Circumference of Circle = %f\n", circum ) ;
    return 0 ;
}
```

(c) Paper of size A0 has dimensions 1189 mm x 841 mm. Each subsequent size A(n) is defined as A(n-1) cut in half, parallel to its shorter sides. Write a program to calculate and print paper sizes A0, A1, A2, ... A8.

*Program:*

```
/* Calculation of Paper Sizes A0 to A8 */
# include <stdio.h>
int main( )
{
    int a0ht, a0wd ;
    int a1ht, a1wd, a2ht, a2wd, a3ht, a3wd, a4ht, a4wd ;
    int a5ht, a5wd, a6ht, a6wd, a7ht, a7wd, a8ht, a8wd ;
    a0ht = 1189 ; a0wd = 841 ;
    printf ( "Size of A0 paper Ht = %d Width = %d\n", a0ht, a0wd ) ;
    a1ht = a0wd ; a1wd = a0ht / 2 ;
    printf ( "Size of A1 paper Ht = %d Width = %d\n", a1ht, a1wd ) ;
    a2ht = a1wd ; a2wd = a1ht / 2 ;
    printf ( "Size of A2 paper Ht = %d Width = %d\n", a2ht, a2wd ) ;
    a3ht = a2wd ; a3wd = a2ht / 2 ;
    printf ( "Size of A3 paper Ht = %d Width = %d\n", a3ht, a3wd ) ;
    a4ht = a3wd ; a4wd = a3ht / 2 ;
    printf ( "Size of A4 paper Ht = %d Width = %d\n", a4ht, a4wd ) ;
    a5ht = a4wd ; a5wd = a4ht / 2 ;
    printf ( "Size of A5 paper Ht = %d Width = %d\n", a5ht, a5wd ) ;
    a6ht = a5wd ; a6wd = a5ht / 2 ;
    printf ( "Size of A6 paper Ht = %d Width = %d\n", a6ht, a6wd ) ;
    a7ht = a6wd ; a7wd = a6ht / 2 ;
    printf ( "Size of A7 paper Ht = %d Width = %d\n", a7ht, a7wd ) ;
    a8ht = a7wd ; a8wd = a7ht / 2 ;
    printf ( "Size of A8 paper Ht = %d Width = %d\n", a8ht, a8wd ) ;
    return 0 ;
}
```

# CHAPTER
# TWO

# C Instructions

**[A]** Point out the errors, if any, in the following C statements:

(a) x = ( y + 3 ) ;

No error.

(b) cir = 2 * 3.141593 * r ;

No error.

(c) char = '3' ;

Error. Keyword cannot be used as a variable name.

(d) 4 / 3 * 3.14 * r * r * r = vol_of_sphere ;

Error. On the left-hand side of equal to (=) there can only be a variable.

(e) volume = $a^3$ ;

Error. $a^3$ is not a valid statement. Instead, we can use a * a * a.

(f) area = 1 / 2 * base * height ;

No error.

(g) si = p * r * n / 100 ;

No error.

(h) area of circle = 3.14 * r * r ;

Error. **area of circle** is an invalid variable name.

(i) peri_of_tri = a + b + c ;

No error.

(j) slope = ( y2 - y1 ) ÷ ( x2 - x1 ) ;

Error. '÷' is an invalid operator.

(k) 3 = b = 4 = a ;

Error. A variable name must be present on the left hand side of '=' operator.

(l) count = count + 1 ;

No error.

(m) char ch = '25 Apr 12' ;

Error. Multiple characters cannot be stored in a char variable.

**[B]** Evaluate the following expressions and show their hierarchy.

(a) ans = 5 * b * b * x - 3 * a * y * y - 8 * b * b * x + 10 * a * y ;

(a = 3, b = 2, x = 5, y = 4 assume **ans** to be a int)

*Answer:*

| | |
|---|---|
| ans = **5 * 2** * 2 * 5 - 3 * 3 * 4 * 4 - 8 * 2 * 2 * 5 + 10 * 3 *4 | operation: * |
| ans = **10 * 2** * 5 - 3 * 3 * 4 * 4 - 8 * 2 * 2 * 5 + 10 * 3 * 4 | operation: * |
| ans = **20 * 5** - 3 * 3 * 4 * 4 - 8 * 2 * 2 * 5 + 10 * 3 * 4 | operation: * |
| ans = 100 - **3 * 3** * 4 * 4 - 8 * 2 * 2 * 5 + 10 * 3 * 4 | operation: * |
| ans = 100 - **9 * 4** * 4 - 8 * 2 * 2 * 5 + 10 * 3 * 4 | operation: * |
| ans = 100 - **36 * 4** - 8 * 2 * 2 * 5 + 10 * 3 * 4 | operation: * |
| ans = 100 - 144 - **8 * 2** * 2 * 5 + 10 * 3 * 4 | operation: * |
| ans = 100 - 144 - **16 * 2** * 5 + 10 * 3 * 4 | operation: * |
| ans = 100 - 144 - **32 * 5** + 10 * 3 * 4 | operation: * |
| ans = 100 - 144 - 160 + **10 * 3** * 4 | operation: * |
| ans = 100 - 144 - 160 + **30 * 4** | operation: * |
| ans = **100 - 144** - 160 + 120 | operation: - |
| ans = **-44 - 160** + 120 | operation: - |
| ans = **-204 + 120** | operation: + |
| ans = -84 | |

(b) res = 4 * a * y / c - a * y / c ;

(a = 4, y = 1, c = 3, assume **res** to be an int)

*Answer:*

| | |
|---|---|
| res = **4 * 4** * 1 / 3 - 4 * 1 / 3 | operation: * |
| res = **16 * 1** / 3 - 4 * 1 / 3 | operation: * |

res = **16 / 3** - 4 * 1 / 3 operation: /
res = 5 - **4 * 1** / 3 operation: *
res = 5 - **4 / 3** operation: /
res = **5 - 1** operation: -
res = 4

(c) s = c + a * y * y / b ;

(a = 2.2, b = 0.0, c = 4.1, y = 3.0, assume **s** to be a float)

*Answer:*

s = 4.1 + **2.2 * 3.0** * 3.0 / 0.0 operation: *
s = 4.1 + **6.6 * 3.0** / 0.0 operation: *
s = 4.1 + **19.8 / 0.0** operation: /
Here we cannot Divide by 0

(d) R = x * x + 2 * x + 1 / 2 * x * x + x + 1 ;

(x = 3.5, assume **R** to be a float)

*Answer:*

R = **3.5 * 3.5** + 2 * 3.5 + 1 / 2 * 3.5 * 3.5 + 3.5 + 1 operation: *
R = 12.25 + **2 * 3.5** + 1 / 2 * 3.5 * 3.5 + 3.5 + 1 operation: *
R = 12.25 + 7.0 + 1 / **2 * 3.5** * 3.5 + 3.5 + 1 operation: *
R = 12.25 + 7.0 + 1 / **7.0 * 3.5** + 3.5 + 1 operation: *
R = 12.25 + 7.0 + **1 / 24.5** + 3.5 + 1 operation: /
R = **12.25 + 7.0** + 0.04081 + 3.5 + 1 operation: +
R = **19.25 + 0.04081** + 3.5 + 1 operation: +
R = **19.29081 + 3.5** + 1 operation: +
R = **22.79081 + 1** operation: +
S = 23.79081

**[C]** Indicate the order in which the following expressions would be evaluated.

(a) g = 10 / 5 / 2 / 1 ;

Evaluation order would be:

g = **10 / 5** / 2 / 1 ; operation: /
g = **2 / 2** / 1 ; operation: /
g = **1 / 1** ; operation: /
g = 1 ; operation: =

(b) b = 3 / 2 + 5 * 4 / 3 ;

Evaluation order would be:

| | |
|---|---|
| b = **3 / 2** + 5 * 4 / 3 | operation: / |
| b = 1 + **5 * 4** / 3 | operation: * |
| b = 1 + **20 / 3** | operation: / |
| b = **1 + 6** | operation: + |
| b = 7 | operation: = |

(c) a = b = c = 3 + 4 ;

Evaluation order would be:

| | |
|---|---|
| a = b = c = **3 + 4** | operation: + |
| a = b = **c = 7** | operation: = |
| a = **b = 7** | operation: = |
| a = 7 | operation: = |

(d) x = 2 - 3 + 5 * 2 / 8 % 3 ;

Evaluation order would be:

| | |
|---|---|
| x = 2 - 3 + **5 * 2** / 8 % 3 | operation: * |
| x = 2 - 3 + **10 / 8** % 3 | operation: / |
| x = 2 - 3 + **1 % 3** | operation: % |
| x = **2 - 3** + 1 | operation: - |
| x = **-1 + 1** | operation: + |
| x = 0 | operation: = |

(e) z = 5 % 3 / 8 * 3 + 4 ;

Evaluation order would be:

| | |
|---|---|
| z = **5 % 3** / 8 * 3 + 4 | operation: % |
| z = **2 / 8** * 3 + 4 | operation: / |
| z = **0 * 3** + 4 | operation: * |
| z = **0 + 4** | operation: + |
| z = 4 | operation: = |

(f) y = z = -3 % -8 / 2 + 7 ;

Evaluation order would be:

| | |
|---|---|
| y = z = **-3** % -8 / 2 + 7 | operation: - |
| y = z = -3 % **-8** / 2 + 7 | operation: - |
| y = z = **-3 % -8** / 2 + 7 | operation: % |

```
y = z = -3 / 2 + 7                    operation: /
y = z = -1 + 7                        operation: +
y = z = 6                             operation: =
y = 6                                 operation: =
```

**[D]** What will be the output of the following programs?

(a)
```
# include <stdio.h>
int main( )
{
    int  i = 2, j = 3, k, l ;
    float  a, b ;
    k = i / j * j ;
    l = j / i * i ;
    a = i / j * j ;
    b = j / i * i ;
    printf ( "%d %d %f %f\n", k, l, a, b ) ;
    return 0 ;
}
```

*Output:*

```
0 2 0.000000 2.000000
```

(b)
```
# include <stdio.h>
int main( )
{
    int  a, b, c, d ;
    a = 2 % 5 ;
    b = -2 % 5 ;
    c = 2 % -5 ;
    d = -2 % -5 ;
    printf ( "a = %d b = %d c = %d d = %d\n", a, b, c, d ) ;
    return 0 ;
}
```

*Output:*

```
a = 2  b = -2  c = 2  d = -2
```

(c)
```
# include <stdio.h>
int main( )
{
    float a = 5,  b = 2 ;
```

```
    int c, d ;
    c = a % b ;
    d = a / 2 ;
    printf ( "%d\n", d ) ;
    return 0 ;
}
```

*Output:*

Error. Mod ( % ) operator cannot be used on **floats**

(d)
```
# include <stdio.h>
int main( )
{
    printf ( "nn \n\n nn\n" ) ;
    printf ( "nn /n/n nn/n" ) ;
    return 0 ;
}
```

*Output:*

```
nn

 nn
nn /n/n nn/n
```

(e)
```
# include <stdio.h>
int main( )
{
    int a, b ;
    printf ( "Enter values of a and b" ) ;
    scanf ( " %d %d ", &a, &b ) ;
    printf ( "a  = %d b = %d", a, b ) ;
    return 0 ;
}
```

*Output:*

Since spaces are given after and before double quotes in **scanf( )** we must supply a space, then two numbers and again a space followed by enter. The **printf( )** would then output the two number that you enter.

**[E]** State whether the following statements are True or False:

(a) * or /, + or - represents the correct hierarchy of arithmetic operators in C.

Answer: True

(b) [ ] and { } can be used in Arithmetic instructions.

Answer: False

(c) Hierarchy decides which operator is used first.

Answer: True

(d) In C, Arithmetic instruction cannot contain constants on left side of =.

Answer: True

(e) In C ** operator is used for exponentiation operation.

Answer: False

(f) % operator cannot be used on floats.

Answer: True

**[F]** Fill in the blanks:

(a) In y = 10 * x / 2 + z ; 10 * x operation will be performed first.

(b) If **a** is an integer variable, a = 11 / 2 would store 5 in **a**.

(c) The expression, a = 22 / 7 * 5 / 3 would evaluate to 5.

(d) The expression x = -7 % 2 - 8 would evaluate to -9.

(e) If **d** is a **float** the operation **d = 2 / 7.0** would store 0.285714 in **d**.

**[G]** Attempt the following questions:

(a) If a five-digit number is input through the keyboard, write a program to calculate the sum of its digits. (Hint: Use the modulus operator **%**)

*Program:*

```
/* Obtain sum of digits of a 5-digit number */
# include <stdio.h>
int main( )
{
    int  num, a, n ;
    int  sum = 0 ;
    printf ( "\nEnter a 5 digit number (less than 32767): " ) ;
    scanf ( "%d", &num ) ;
    a = num % 10 ;        /* 5th digit extracted as remainder */
    n = num / 10 ;        /* remaining digits */
    sum = sum + a ;       /* sum updated by adding extracted digit */
    a = n % 10 ;          /* 4th digit */
    n = n / 10 ;
    sum = sum + a ;
    a = n % 10 ;          /* 3rd digit */
    n = n / 10 ;
    sum = sum + a ;
    a = n % 10 ;          /* 2nd digit */
    n = n / 10 ;
    sum = sum + a ;
    a = n % 10 ;          /* 1st digit */
    sum = sum + a ;
    printf ( "Sum of 5 digits of %d is %d\n", num, sum ) ;
    return 0 ;
}
```

(b) Write a program to receive Cartesian co-ordinates (x, y) of a point and convert them into polar co-ordinates (r, φ).

*Program:*

```
/* Convert Cartesian co-ordinates to Polar co-ordinates  */
# include <stdio.h>
# include <math.h>
int main( )
{
    float  x, y, r, theta ;
    printf ( "\nEnter x and y co-ordinates: " ) ;
    scanf ( "%f %f", &x, &y ) ;
```

```
    r = sqrt ( x * x + y * y ) ;
    theta = atan2 ( y, x ) ;
    theta = theta * 180 / 3.14 ;  /* convert to degrees */
    printf ( "r = %f theta = %f\n", r, theta ) ;
    return 0 ;
}
```

(c) Write a program to receive values of latitude (L1, L2) and longitude (G1, G2), in degrees, of two places on the earth and outputs the distance between them in nautical miles. The formula for distance in nautical miles is:

D = 3963 acos ( sin L1 sin L2 + cos L1cos L2 * cos ( G2 – G1 )

*Program:*

```
/* Calculate distance between two places in Nautical Miles */
# include <stdio.h>
# include <math.h>
int main( )
{
    float lat1, lat2, lon1, lon2, d ;
    printf ( "\nEnter Latitude and Longitude of Place 1: " ) ;
    scanf ( "%f %f", &lat1, &lon1 ) ;
    printf ( "Enter Latitude and Longitude of Place 2: " ) ;
    scanf ( "%f %f", &lat2, &lon2 ) ;
    lat1 = lat1 * 3.14 / 180 ;
    lat2 = lat2 * 3.14 / 180 ;
    lon1 = lon1 * 3.14 / 180 ;
    lon2 = lon2 * 3.14 / 180 ;
    d = 3963 * acos ( sin ( lat1 ) * sin ( lat2 ) + cos ( lat1 ) * cos ( lat2 )
        * cos ( lon2 - lon1 ) ) ;
    printf ( "Distance between Place1 and Place 2: %f\n", d ) ;
    return 0 ;
}
```

(d) Wind-chill factor is the felt air temperature on exposed skin due to wind. The wind-chill temperature is always lower than the air temperature, and is calculated as per the following formula:

$wcf = 35.74 + 0.6215t + ( 0.4275t - 35.75 ) * v^{0.16}$

where **t** is the temperature and **v** is the wind velocity. Write a program to receive values of **t** and **v** and calculate wind-chill factor.

*Program:*

```
/* Calculation of wind chill factor */
# include <stdio.h>
# include <math.h>
int main( )
{
    float  temp, vel, wcf ;
    printf ( "\nEnter values of temp and velocity: " ) ;
    scanf ( "%f %f", &temp, &vel ) ;
    wcf = 35.74 + 0.6215 * temp + ( 0.4275 * temp - 35.75 )
               * pow ( vel, 0.16f ) ;
    printf ( "Wind Chill Factor = %f\n", wcf ) ;
    return 0 ;
}
```

(e) If value of an angle is input through the keyboard, write a program to print all its Trigonometric ratios.

*Program:*

```
/* Print all Trignometric ratios of an angle */
# include <stdio.h>
# include <math.h>

int main( )
{
    float angle, s, c, t ;
    printf ( "\nEnter an angle: " ) ;
    scanf ( "%f", &angle ) ;
    /* convert angle to radians */
    angle = angle * 3.14 / 180 ;
    s =  sin ( angle ) ;
    c = cos ( angle ) ;
    t = tan ( angle ) ;
    printf ( "sin = %f cos = %f tan = %f\n", s, c, t ) ;
    return 0 ;
}
```

(f) Two numbers are input through the keyboard into two locations C and D. Write a program to interchange the contents of C and D.

*Program:*

```
/* Interchanging of contents of two variables c & d */
# include <stdio.h>

int main( )
{
    int  c, d, e ;
    printf ( "\nEnter the number at location C: " ) ;
    scanf ( "%d", &c ) ;
    printf ( "\nEnter the number at location D: " ) ;
    scanf ( "%d", &d ) ;
    e = c ;
    c = d ;
    d = e ;
    printf ( "New Number at location C = %d\n", c ) ;
    printf ( "New Number at location D = %d\n", d ) ;
    return 0 ;
}
```

# CHAPTER
# THREE

# Decision Control Instruction

**[A]** What will be the output of the following programs?

(a)
```
# include <stdio.h>
int main( )
{
   int  a = 300, b, c ;
   if ( a >= 400 )
       b = 300 ;
   c = 200 ;
   printf ( "%d %d\n", b, c ) ;
   return 0 ;
}
```

*Output:*

**b** will contain some garbage value and **c** will be equal to 200

(b)
```
# include <stdio.h>
int main( )
{
   int  x = 10, y = 20 ;
   if ( x == y ) ;
       printf ( "%d %d\n", x, y ) ;
   return 0 ;
}
```

*Output:*

10 20

(c)
```
# include <stdio.h>
```

```
int main( )
{
   int  x = 3 ;
   float  y = 3.0 ;
   if ( x == y )
       printf ( "x and y are equal\n" ) ;
   else
       printf ( "x and y are not equal\n" ) ;
   return 0 ;
}
```

*Output:*

x and y are equal

(d)
```
# include <stdio.h>
int main( )
{
   int  x = 3, y, z ;
   y = x = 10 ;
   z = x < 10 ;
   printf ( "x = %d y = %d z = %d\n", x, y, z ) ;
   return 0 ;
}
```

*Output:*

x = 10  y = 10  z = 0

(e)
```
# include <stdio.h>
int main( )
{
   int i = 65 ;
   char j = 'A' ;
   if ( i == j )
       printf ( "C is WOW\n" ) ;
   else
       printf( "C is a headache\n" ) ;
   return 0 ;
}
```

*Output:*

C is WOW

**[B]** Point out the errors, if any, in the following programs:

(a)
```
# include <stdio.h>
int main( )
{
   float a = 12.25, b = 12.52 ;
   if ( a = b )
       printf ( "a and b are equal\n" ) ;
   return 0 ;
}
```

No Error. 12.52 would get assigned to **a**, condition would be evaluated to true and **printf( )** would get executed.

(b)
```
# include <stdio.h>
int main( )
{
   int j = 10, k = 12 ;
   if ( k >= j )
   {
       {
           k = j ;
           j = k ;
       }
   }
   return 0 ;
}
```

No Error. Any number of pairs of braces can be used.

(c)
```
# include <stdio.h>
int main( )
{
   if ( 'X' < 'x' )
       printf ( "ascii value of X is smaller than that of x\n" ) ;
}
```

No Error. ASCII values of x and X are being compared.

(d)
```
# include <stdio.h>
int main( )
{
   int  x = 10 ;
   if ( x >= 2 ) then
       printf ( "%d\n", x ) ;
```

```
    return 0 ;
}
```

Error. 'then' cannot be used in C.

(e)
```
# include <stdio.h>
int main( )
{
    int x = 10, y = 15 ;
    if ( x % 2 = y % 3 )
        printf ( "Carpathians\n" ) ;
    return 0 ;
}
```

Error. For comparison use == and not =.

(f)
```
# include <stdio.h>
int main( )
{
    int a, b ;
    scanf ( "%d %d", a, b ) ;
    if ( a > b ) ;
        printf ( "This is a game\n" ) ;
    else
        printf ( "You have to play it\n" ) ;
    return 0 ;
}
```

**[C]** State whether the following statements are True or False:

(a) ; is a valid statement.

Answer: True

(b) Ifs can be nested.

Answer: True

(c) If there are multiple statements in if or else block they should be enclosed within a pair of { }.

Answer: True

(d) If can occur within an if block but not in the else block.

Answer: False

(e) By default there is only one statement in if block and only one in the else block.

Answer: True

(f) Nothing happens on execution of a null statement.

Answer: True

**[D]** Match the following pairs:

| | |
|---|---|
| (a) Multiples statements | (1) { } |
| (b) else block | (2) optional |
| (c) ; | (3) Null statement |
| (d) < > <= >= == != | (4) Relational operators |
| (e) == | (5) Comparison operator |
| (f) + - * / % | (6) Arithmetic operators |
| (g) = | (7) Assignment operator |
| (h) Default control instruction | (8) Sequence |
| (i) Decision control instruction | (9) if - else |

**[E]** Which of the following are valid ifs:

(a) if ( -25)

(b) if ( 3.14 )

(c) if ( a )

(d) if ( a + b )

(e) if ( a >= b )

Answer: (a), (b), (c), (d), (e)

**[F]** Attempt the following questions:

(a) A five-digit number is entered through the keyboard. Write a program to obtain the reversed number and to determine whether the original and reversed numbers are equal or not.

*Program:*

```
/* Check whether a number and its reversed number are equal */
# include <stdio.h>
int main( )
{
```

```
    int  n, a, b, num ;
    long int  revnum = 0 ;
    printf ( "\nEnter a 5-digit number <= 32767): " ) ;
    scanf ( "%d", &n ) ;
    num = n ;
    a = n % 10 ;  /* last digit */
    n = n / 10 ;  /* remaining digits */
    revnum = revnum + a * 10000L;
    a = n % 10 ;  /* 4 th digit */
    n = n / 10 ;  /* remaining digits */
    revnum = revnum + a * 1000;
    a = n % 10 ;  /* 3 rd digit */
    n = n / 10 ;  /* remaining digits */
    revnum = revnum + a * 100;
    a = n % 10 ;  /* 2 nd digit */
    n = n / 10 ;  /* remaining digits */
    revnum = revnum + a * 10 ;
    a = n % 10 ;  /* 1 st digit */
    revnum = revnum + a ;
    if ( revnum == num )
        printf ( "Given no. & its reversed number are equal\n" ) ;
    else
        printf ( "Given no. & its reversed number are not equal\n" ) ;
    return 0 ;
}
```

(b) If ages of Ram, Shyam and Ajay are input through the keyboard, write a program to determine the youngest of the three.

*Program:*

```
/* Find the youngest amongst three friends */
# include <stdio.h>
int main( )
{
    int r, s, a, young ;
    printf ( "\nEnter age of Ram, Shyam and Ajay: " ) ;
    scanf ( "%d %d %d", &r, &s, &a ) ;
    if ( r < s )
    {
        if ( r < a )
            young = r ;
```

```
            else
                young = a ;
        }
        else
        {
            if ( s < a )
                young = s ;
            else
                young = a ;
        }
        printf ( "The youngest of Ram(%d), Shyam(%d) and Ajay(%d) is
                %d\n", r, s, a, young ) ;
        return 0 ;
    }
```

(c) Write a program to check whether a triangle is valid or not, if three angles of the triangle are entered through the keyboard. A triangle is valid if the sum of all the three angles is equal to 180 degrees.

*Program:*

```
/* Check whether a triangle is valid or not */
# include <stdio.h>
int main( )
{
    float  angle1, angle2, angle3 ;
    printf ( "\nEnter three angles of the triangle: " ) ;
    scanf ( "%f %f %f", &angle1, &angle2, &angle3 ) ;
    if ( ( angle1 + angle2 + angle3 ) == 180 )
        printf ( "The triangle is a valid triangle\n" ) ;
    else
    printf ( "The triangle is an invalid triangle\n" ) ;
    return 0 ;
}
```

(d) Write a program to find the absolute value of a number entered through the keyboard.

*Program:*

```
/* To find absolute value of number entered through keyboard*/
# include <stdio.h>
int main( )
```

```
{
    int no ;
    printf ( "\nEnter any number: " ) ;
    scanf ( "%d", &no ) ;
    if ( no < 0 )
        no = no * -1 ;
    printf ( "The absolute value of given number is %d\n", no ) ;
    return 0 ;
}
```

(e) Given the length and breadth of a rectangle, write a program to find whether the area of the rectangle is greater than its perimeter. For example, the area of the rectangle with length = 5 and breadth = 4 is greater than its perimeter.

*Program:*

```
/* Find whether area of rectangle is greater than its perimeter */
# include <stdio.h>
int main( )
{
    int l, b, area, peri ;
    printf ( "\nEnter length and breadth of the rectangle: " ) ;
    scanf ( "%d %d", &l, &b ) ;
    area = l * b ;
    peri = 2 * ( l + b ) ;
    if ( area > peri )
        printf ( "area is greater than perimeter\n" ) ;
    else
        printf ( "area is lesser than perimeter\n" ) ;

    return 0 ;
}
```

(f) Given three points **(x1, y1)**, **(x2, y2)** and **(x3, y3)**, write a program to check if the three points fall on one straight line.

*Program:*

```
/* Check whether three points are co-linear */
# include <stdio.h>
# include <math.h>
int main( )
```

```
{
    int  x1, y1, x2, y2, x3, y3 ;
    int  s1, s2, s3 ;
    printf ( "\nEnter the values of x1 and y1 coord. of first point: " ) ;
    scanf ( "%d%d", &x1, &y1 ) ;
    printf ( "\nEnter the values of x2 and y2 coord. of first point: " ) ;
    scanf ( "%d%d", &x2, &y2 ) ;
    printf ( "\nEnter the values of x3 and y3 coord. of first point: " ) ;
    scanf ( "%d%d", &x3, &y3 ) ;
    /* Calculate Slope of line between each pair of points */
    s1 = abs ( x2- x1 ) / abs ( y2 - y1 ) ;
    s2 = abs ( x3 - x1 ) / abs ( y3 - y1 ) ;
    s3 = abs ( x3 - x2 ) / abs ( y3 - y2 ) ;
    if ( ( s1 == s2 ) && ( s1 == s3 ) )
        printf ( "Points are Co-linear\n" ) ;
    else
        printf ( "Points are NOT Co-linear\n" ) ;
    return 0 ;
}
```

(g) Given the coordinates **(x, y)** of center of a circle and its radius, write a program that will determine whether a point lies inside the circle, on the circle or outside the circle. (Hint: Use **sqrt( )** and **pow( )** functions)

*Program:*

```
/* Determine position of point with respect to a circle */
/* The center of the circle has been assumed to be at (0, 0) */
# include <stdio.h>
int main( )
{
    int  x, y, r ;
    int  dis, d ;
    printf ( "\nEnter radius of circle& coordinates of point ( x, y ): " ) ;
    scanf ( "%d %d %d", &r, &x, &y ) ;
    dis = x * x + y * y ;  /* or use pow( ) function*/
    d = r * r ;
    if ( dis == d )
        printf ( "Point is on the circle\n" ) ;
    else
    {
```

```
        if ( dis > d )
            printf ( "Point is outside the circle\n" ) ;
        else
            printf ( "Point is inside the circle\n" ) ;
    }
    return 0 ;
}
```

(h) Given a point **(x, y)**, write a program to find out if it lies on x-axis, y-axis or origin.

*Program:*

```
/* Determine position of a point with respect to X and Y axes */
# include <stdio.h>
int main( )
{
    int  x, y ;
    printf ( "\nEnter the x and y coordinates of a point: " ) ;
    scanf ( "%d%d", &x, &y ) ;
    if ( x == 0 && y == 0 )
        printf ( "Point lies on origin\n" ) ;
    else
        if ( x == 0 && y != 0 )
            printf ( "Point lies on Y axis\n" ) ;
        else
            if ( x != 0 && y == 0 )
                printf ( "Point  lies on X axis\n" ) ;
            else
                printf ( "Point neither lies on any axis, nor origin\n" );
    return 0 ;
}
```

(i) According to Gregorian calendar, it was Monday on the date 01/01/01. If any year is input through the keyboard write a program to find out what is the day on 1st January of this year.

*Program:*

```
/* Calculate the day on 1st January of any year */
# include <stdio.h>
int main( )
{
```

```
    int leapdays, firstday, yr ;
    long int normaldays, totaldays ;
    printf ( "Enter year:" ) ;
    scanf ( "%d", &yr );
    normaldays = ( yr - 1 ) * 365L ;
    leapdays = ( yr - 1 ) / 4 - ( yr - 1 ) / 100 + ( yr - 1 ) / 400 ;
    totaldays = normaldays + leapdays ;
    firstday = totaldays % 7 ;
    if ( firstday == 0 )
        printf ( "Monday\n" ) ;
    if ( firstday == 1 )
        printf ( "Tuesday\n" ) ;
    if ( firstday == 2 )
        printf ( "Wednesday\n" ) ;
    if ( firstday == 3 )
        printf ( "Thursday\n" ) ;
    if ( firstday == 4 )
        printf ( "Friday\n" ) ;
    if ( firstday == 5 )
        printf ( "Saturday\n" ) ;
    if ( firstday == 6 )
        printf ( "Sunday\n" ) ;
    return 0 ;
}
```

# CHAPTER FOUR

# More Complex Decision Making

**[A]** If a = 10, b = 12, c = 0, find the values of the expressions in the following table:

| **Expression** | **Value** |
|---|---|
| a != 6 && b > 5 | 1 |
| a == 9 \|\| b < 3 | 0 |
| ! ( a < 10 ) | 1 |
| ! ( a > 5 && c ) | 1 |
| 5 && c != 8 \|\| !c | 1 |

**[B]** What will be the output of the following programs?

(a)
```
# include <stdio.h>
int main( )
{
    int  i = 4, z = 12 ;
    if ( i = 5 || z > 50 )
        printf ( "Dean of students affairs\n" ) ;
    else
        printf ( "Dosa\n" ) ;
    return 0 ;
}
```

*Output:*

Dean of students affairs

(b)
```
# include <stdio.h>
int main( )
{
    int  i = 4, j = -1, k = 0, w, x, y, z ;
    w = i || j || k ;
    x = i && j && k ;
    y = i || j && k ;
    z = i && j || k ;
    printf ( "w = %d x = %d y = %d z = %d\n", w, x, y, z ) ;
    return 0 ;
}
```

*Output:*

w = 1  x = 0  y = 1  z = 1

(c)
```
# include <stdio.h>
int main( )
{
    int x = 20, y = 40, z = 45 ;
    if ( x > y && x > z )
        printf ( "biggest = %d\n", x ) ;
    else if ( y > x && y > z )
        printf ( "biggest = %d\n", y ) ;
    else if ( z > x && z > y )
        printf ( "biggest = %d\n", z ) ;
    return 0 ;
}
```

*Output:*

biggest = 45

(d)
```
# include <stdio.h>
int main( )
{
    int  i = -4, j, num ;
    j = ( num < 0 ? 0 : num * num ) ;
    printf ( "%d\n", j ) ;
    return 0 ;
}
```

*Output:*

Unpredictable. **num** not initialised

(e)
```
# include <stdio.h>
int main( )
{
    int  k, num = 30 ;
    k = ( num > 5 ? ( num <= 10 ? 100 : 200 ) : 500 ) ;
    printf ( "%d\n", num ) ;
    return 0 ;
}
```

*Output:*

30

**[C]** Point out the errors, if any, in the following programs:

(a)
```
# include <stdio.h>
int main( )
{
    char   spy = 'a', password = 'z' ;
    if ( spy == 'a' or password == 'z' )
        printf ( "All the birds are safe in the nest\n" ) ;
    return 0 ;
}
```

Error. 'or' cannot be used to combine conditions. Use ||.

(b)
```
# include <stdio.h>
int main( )
{
    int   i = 10, j = 20 ;
    if ( i = 5 ) && if ( j = 10 )
        printf ( "Have a nice day\n" ) ;
    return 0 ;
}
```

Error. Condition should be *if ( i == 5 && j == 10 )*.

(c)
```
# include <stdio.h>
int main( )
{
```

```
    int x = 10, y = 20 ;
    if ( x >= 2  and  y <= 50 ) ;
        printf ( "%d\n", x ) ;
    return 0 ;
}
```

Error. Replace and with && to combine the conditions.

(d)
```
# include <stdio.h>
int main( )
{
    int x = 2 ;
    if ( x == 2 && x != 0 ) ;
        printf ( "Hello\n" ) ;
    else
        printf ( "Bye\n" ) ;
    return 0 ;
}
```

Error. The **if** statement should not be terminated by a semicolon.

(e)
```
# include <stdio.h>
int main( )
{
    int j = 65 ;
    printf ( "j >= 65 ? %d : %c\n", j ) ;
    return 0 ;
}
```

No Error.

(f)
```
# include <stdio.h>
int main( )
{
    int  i = 10, j ;
    i >= 5 ?  j = 10 :  j = 15 ;
    printf ( "%d %d\n", i, j ) ;
    return 0 ;
}
```

Error. lvalue required. Parenthesize j = 10 and j = 15 to eliminate the error.

(g)
```
# include <stdio.h>
int main( )
{
    int a = 5, b = 6 ;
    ( a == b ? printf ( "%d\n", a ) ) ;
    return 0 ;
}
```

Error. The ? operator must have a matching : operator.

(h)
```
# include <stdio.h>
int main( )
{
    int n = 9 ;
    ( n == 9 ? printf ( "Correct\n" ) ; : printf ( "Wrong\n" ) ; ) ;
    return 0 ;
}
```

Error. Remove the ; after each **printf( )**.

**[D]** Attempt the following questions:

(a) If the lengths of three sides of a triangle are entered through the keyboard, write a program to check whether the triangle is an isosceles, an equilateral, a scalene or a right-angled triangle.

*Program:*

```
/* Determine the type of triangle */
# include <stdio.h>
int main( )
{
    int s1, s2, s3, a, b, c ;
    printf ( "\nEnter three sides of a triangle: " ) ;
    scanf ( "%d %d %d", &s1, &s2, &s3 ) ;
    if ( s1 != s2 && s2 != s3 && s3 != s1 )
        printf ( "Scalene triangle\n" ) ;
    if ( ( s1 == s2 ) && ( s2 != s3 ) )
        printf ( "Isosceles triangle\n" ) ;
    if ( ( s2 == s3 ) && ( s3 != s1 ) )
        printf ( "Isosceles triangle\n" ) ;
```

```
    if ( ( s1 == s3 ) && ( s3 != s2 ) )
        printf ( "Isosceles triangle\n" ) ;
    if ( s1 == s2 && s2 == s3 )
        printf ( "Equilateral triangle\n" ) ;
    a = ( s1 * s1 ) == ( s2 * s2 ) + ( s3 * s3 ) ;
    b = ( s2 * s2 ) == ( s1 * s1 ) + ( s3 * s3 ) ;
    c = ( s3 * s3 ) == ( s1 * s1 ) + ( s2 * s2 ) ;
    if ( a || b || c )
        printf ( "Right-angled triangle\n" ) ;
    return 0 ;
}
```

(b) In digital world colors are specified in Red-Green-Blue (RGB) format, with values of R, G, B varying on an integer scale from 0 to 255. In print publishing the colors are mentioned in Cyan-Magenta-Yellow-Black (CMYK) format, with values of C, M, Y, and K varying on a real scale from 0.0 to 1.0. Write a program that converts RGB color to CMYK color as per the following formulae:

$$White = Max(Red / 255, Green / 255, Blue / 255)$$

$$Cyan = \left( \frac{White - Red / 255}{White} \right)$$

$$\text{Magenta} = \left( \frac{White - Green / 255}{White} \right)$$

$$Yellow = \left( \frac{White - Blue / 255}{White} \right)$$

$$Black = 1 - White$$

Note that if the RGB values are all 0, then the CMY values are all 0 and the K value is 1.

*Program:*

```
/* Color conversion from RGB to CMYK format */
# include <stdio.h>
int main( )
{
```

```
    float red, green, blue ;
    float white, cyan, magenta, yellow, black ;
    float max ;
    printf ( "\nEnter Red, Green, Blue values (0 to 255): " ) ;
    scanf ( "%f %f %f", &red, &green, &blue ) ;
    if ( red == 0 && green == 0 && blue == 0 )
    {
        cyan = magenta = yellow = 0 ;
        black = 1 ;
    }
    else
    {
        red = red / 255 ;
        green = green / 255 ;
        blue = blue / 255 ;
        max = red ;
        if ( green > max )
            max = green ;
        if ( blue > max )
            max = blue ;
        white = max ;
        cyan = ( white - red ) / white ;
        magenta = ( white - green ) / white ;
        yellow = ( white - blue ) / white ;
        black = 1 - white ;
    }
    printf ( "CMYK = %f %f %f %f\n", cyan, magenta, yellow, black ) ;
    return 0 ;
}
```

(c) A certain grade of steel is graded according to the following conditions:

(i) Hardness must be greater than 50
(ii) Carbon content must be less than 0.7
(iii) Tensile strength must be greater than 5600

The grades are as follows:

Grade is 10 if all three conditions are met
Grade is 9 if conditions (i) and (ii) are met
Grade is 8 if conditions (ii) and (iii) are met
Grade is 7 if conditions (i) and (iii) are met

Grade is 6 if only one condition is met
Grade is 5 if none of the conditions are met

Write a program, which will require the user to give values of hardness, carbon content and tensile strength of the steel under consideration and output the grade of the steel.

*Program:*

```
/* Check the grade of steel */
# include <stdio.h>
# include <stdlib.h>
int main( )
{
    float  hard, carbon, tensile ;
    printf ( "\nEnter Hardness of steel: " ) ;
    scanf ( "%f", &hard ) ;
    printf ( "\nEnter Carbon content: " ) ;
    scanf ( "%f", &carbon ) ;
    printf ( "\nEnter Tensile strength:" ) ;
    scanf ( "%f", &tensile ) ;
    if ( hard > 50 && carbon < 0.7 && tensile > 5600 )
    {
        printf ( "Grade 10\n" ) ;
        exit ( 0 ) ;  /* Terminates the execution */
    }
    if ( hard > 50 && carbon < 0.7 && tensile <= 5600 )
    {
        printf ( "Grade 9\n" ) ;
        exit ( 0 ) ;
    }
    if ( hard <= 50 && carbon < 0.7 && tensile > 5600 )
    {
        printf ( "Grade 8\n" ) ;
        exit ( 0 ) ;
    }
    if ( hard > 50 && carbon >= 0.7 && tensile > 5600 )
    {
        printf ( "Grade 7\n" ) ;
        exit ( 0 ) ;
    }
    if ( hard > 50 || carbon < 0.7 || tensile > 5600 )
```

```
    {
        printf ( "Grade 6\n" ) ;
        exit ( 0 ) ;
    }
    printf ( "Grade 5\n" ) ;
    return 0 ;
}
```

(d) The Body Mass Index (BMI) is defined as ratio of the weight of a person (in kilograms) to the square of the height (in meters). Write a program that receives weight and height, calculates the BMI, and reports the BMI category as per the following table:

| **BMI Category** | **BMI** |
|---|---|
| Starvation | < 15 |
| Anorexic | 15.1 to 17.5 |
| Underweight | 17.6 to 18.5 |
| Ideal | 18.6 to 24.9 |
| Overweight | 25 to 25.9 |
| Obese | 30 to 30.9 |
| Morbidly Obese | >= 40 |

*Program:*

```
/* Determine BMI category */
# include <stdio.h>
# include <math.h>
int main( )
{
    float  wt, ht, bmi ;
    printf ( "Enter weight in kg and height in meters: " ) ;
    scanf ( "%f %f", &wt, &ht ) ;
    bmi = wt / ( ht * ht ) ;
    printf ( "Body Mass Index = %f\n", bmi ) ;
    if ( bmi < 15 )
        printf ( "BMI Category: Starvation\n" ) ;
    else if ( bmi < 17.5 )
        printf ( "BMI Category: Anorexic\n" ) ;
    else if ( bmi < 18.5 )
        printf ( "BMI Category: Underweight\n" ) ;
```

```
    else if ( bmi < 25 )
        printf ( "BMI Category: Ideal\n" ) ;
    else if ( bmi < 30 )
        printf ( "BMI Category: Overweight\n" ) ;
    else if ( bmi < 40 )
        printf ( "BMI Category: Obese\n" ) ;
    else
        printf ( "BMI Category: Morbidly Obese\n" ) ;
    return 0 ;
}
```

**[E]** Answer the following questions:

(a) Using conditional operators determine:

(1) Whether the character entered through the keyboard is a lower case alphabet or not.

*Program:*

```
/* Determine character case using conditional operators */
# include <stdio.h>
int main( )
{
    char ch ;
    printf ( "Enter character" ) ;
    scanf ( "%c", &ch ) ;
    ch >= 97 && ch <= 122 ? printf ( "Character is lower
        case\n" ) : printf ( "Character is not lower case\n" ) ;
    return 0 ;
}
```

(2) Whether a character entered through the keyboard is a special symbol or not.

*Program:*

```
/* Determine whether a character is a special symbol */
# include <stdio.h>
int main( )
{
    char ch ;
```

```
    printf ( "Enter character: " ) ;
    scanf ( "%c", &ch ) ;
    ( ( ch >= 0 && ch <= 47 ) || ( ch >= 58 && ch <= 64 ) ||
      ( ch >= 91 && ch <= 96 ) || ( ch >= 123 ) ) ?
          printf ( "Character entered is a special symbol\n" ) :
          printf ( "Character entered is not a special symbol\n" ) ;
    return 0 ;
}
```

(b) Write a program using conditional operators to determine whether a year entered through the keyboard is a leap year or not.

*Program:*

```
/* Determine whether a year is leap or not */
# include <stdio.h>

int main( )
{
    int  year ;
    printf ( "Enter Year: " ) ;
    scanf ( "%d", &year  ) ;
    year % 100 == 0 ? ( year % 400 == 0 ? printf ( " Leap Year\n" )
    : printf ( "Not a Leap Year\n" ) ) : ( year % 4 == 0 ?
    printf ( "Leap Year\n" ) : printf ( "Not A Leap Year\n" ) ) ;
    return 0 ;
}
```

(c) Write a program to find the greatest of three numbers entered through the keyboard. Use conditional operators.

*Program:*

```
/* Determine greatest of 3 numbers using conditional operators */
# include <stdio.h>
int main( )
{
    int n1, n2, n3, great ;
    printf ( "\nEnter three numbers: " ) ;
    scanf ( "%d %d %d", &n1, &n2, &n3 ) ;
    great = n1 > n2 ? ( n1 > n3 ? n1 : n3 ) : ( n2 > n3 ? n2 : n3 ) ;
```

```
    printf ( "Greatest number is: %d\n", great ) ;
    return 0 ;
}
```

(d) Write a program to receive value of an angle in degrees and check whether sum of squares of sine and cosine of this angle is equal to 1.

*Program:*

```
/* Determine whether sum of squares of sine and cosine of an angle
is equal to 1 */
# include <stdio.h>
# include <math.h>
int main( )
{
    int n1, n2, n3 ;
    float angle, sum ;
    printf ( "\nEnter angle in degrees: " ) ;
    scanf ( "%d", &angle ) ;
    angle = angle * 3.14 / 180 ;
    sum = pow ( sin ( angle ), 2 ) + pow ( cos ( angle ), 2 ) ;
    if ( sum == 1 )
        printf ( "sum of squares of sin & cos is equal to 1\n" ) ;
    else
        printf ( "sum of squares of sin & cos is not equal to 1\n" ) ;
    return 0 ;
}
```

(e) Rewrite the following programs using conditional operators.

```
# include <stdio.h>
int main( )
{
    float sal ;
    printf ( "Enter the salary" ) ;
    scanf ( "%f", &sal ) ;
    if ( sal >= 25000 && sal <= 40000 )
        printf ( "Manager\n" ) ;
    else
        if ( sal >= 15000 && sal < 25000 )
            printf ( "Accountant\n" ) ;
```

```
        else
            printf ( "Clerk\n" ) ;
    return 0 ;
}
```

*Program:*

```
# include <stdio.h>
int main( )
{
    float sal ;
    printf ( "Enter the salary" ) ;
    scanf ( "%f", &sal ) ;
    ( sal >= 25000 && sal <= 40000 ? printf ( "Manager\n" ) :
        ( sal >= 15000 && sal < 25000 ? printf ( "Accountant\n" ) :
        printf ( "Clerk\n" ) ) ) ;
    return 0 ;
}
```

# CHAPTER FIVE

# Loop Control Instruction

**[A]** What will be the output of the following programs?

(a)
```
# include <stdio.h>
int main( )
{
    int i = 1 ;
    while ( i <= 10 ) ;
    {
        printf ( "%d\n", i ) ;
        i++ ;
    }
    return 0 ;
}
```

*Output:*

No Output Indefinite while loop because of a ';' at the end of **while**.

(b)
```
# include <stdio.h>
int main( )
{
    int x = 4, y, z ;
    y = --x ;
    z = x-- ;
    printf ( "%d %d %d\n", x, y, z ) ;
    return 0 ;
}
```

*Output:*

2 3 3

(c)
```
# include <stdio.h>
int main( )
{
    int x = 4, y = 3, z ;
    z = x-- - y ;
    printf ( "%d %d %d\n", x, y, z ) ;
    return 0 ;
}
```

*Output:*

3 3 1

(d)
```
# include <stdio.h>
int main( )
{
    while ( 'a' < 'b' )
        printf ( " malayalam is a palindrome\n" ) ;
    return 0 ;
}
```

*Output:*

'malayalam is a palindrome' will be printed indefinitely.

(e)
```
# include <stdio.h>
int main( )
{
    int i ;
    while ( i = 10 )
    {
        printf ( "%d\n", i ) ;
        i = i + 1 ;
    }
    return 0 ;
}
```

*Output:*

**10** will be printed indefinitely.

(f)
```
# include <stdio.h>
int main( )
{
```

```
    float x = 1.1 ;
    while ( x == 1.1 )
    {
        printf ( "%f\n", x ) ;
        x = x - 0.1 ;
    }
    return 0 ;
}
```

*Output:*

No output. Since a **float** variable is compared with **double** constant, condition will not be satisfied.

**[B]** Attempt the following questions:

(a) Write a program to print all the ASCII values and their equivalent characters using a **while** loop. The ASCII values vary from 0 to 255.

*Program:*

```
/* Print ASCII values and their corresponding characters */
# include <stdio.h>
int main( )
{
    int i = 0 ;
    while ( i <= 255 )
    {
        printf ( "%d  %c\n", i, i ) ;
        i++ ;
    }
    return 0 ;
}
```

(b) Write a program to print out all Armstrong numbers between 1 and 500. If sum of cubes of each digit of the number is equal to the number itself, then the number is called an Armstrong number. For example, 153 = ( 1 * 1 * 1 ) + ( 5 * 5 * 5 ) + ( 3 * 3 * 3 ).

*Program:*

```
/* Generate all Armstrong numbers between 1 & 500 */
# include <stdio.h>

int main( )
{
    int i = 1, a, b, c ;
    printf ( "Armstrong numbers between 1 & 500 are:\n" ) ;
    while ( i <= 500 )
    {
        a = i % 10 ; /* extract last digit */
        b = i % 100 ;
        b = ( b - a ) / 10 ; /* extract second digit */
        c = i / 100 ; /* extract first digit */
        if ( ( a * a * a ) + ( b * b * b ) + ( c * c * c ) == i )
            printf ( "%d\n", i ) ;
        i++ ;
    }
    return 0 ;
}
```

(c) Write a program for a matchstick game being played between the computer and a user. Your program should ensure that the computer always wins. Rules for the game are as follows:

- There are 21 matchsticks.
- The computer asks the player to pick 1, 2, 3, or 4 matchsticks.
- After the person picks, the computer does its picking.
- Whoever is forced to pick up the last matchstick loses the game.

*Program:*

```
/* Match stick game */
# include <stdio.h>

int main( )
{
    int m = 21, p, c ;
    while ( 1 )
    {
        printf ( "\n\nNo. of matches left = %d\n", m ) ;
```

```
        printf ( "Pick up 1, 2, 3 or 4 matches: " ) ;
        scanf ( "%d", &p ) ;
        if ( p > 4 || p < 1 )
            continue ;

        m = m - p ;
        printf ( "No. of matches left = %d\n", m ) ;
        c = 5 - p ;
        printf ( "Out of which computer picked up %d\n", c ) ;
        m = m - c ;
        if ( m == 1 )
        {
            printf ( "Number of matches left %d\n\n", m ) ;
            printf ( "You lost the game !!\n" ) ;
            break ;
        }
    }
    return 0 ;
}
```

(d) Write a program to enter numbers till the user wants. At the end it should display the count of positive, negative and zeros entered.

*Program:*

```
/* Count number of positives, negatives and zeros */
# include <stdio.h>
int main( )
{
    int  pos, neg, zero, num ;
    char  ans = 'y' ;
    pos = neg = zero = 0 ;
    while ( ans == 'y' || ans == 'Y' )
    {
        printf ( "\nEnter a number: " ) ;
        scanf ( "%d", &num ) ;
        if ( num == 0 )
            zero++ ;
        if ( num > 0 )
            pos++ ;
        if ( num < 0 )
```

```
            neg++ ;
        fflush ( stdin ) ; // clears standard input stream
        printf ( "\nDo you want to continue? " ) ;
        scanf ( "%c", &ans ) ;
    }
    printf ( "You entered %d positive number(s)\n", pos ) ;
    printf ( "You entered %d negative number(s)\n", neg ) ;
    printf ( "You entered %d zero(s)\n", zero ) ;
    return 0 ;
}
```

(e) Write a program to receive an integer and find its octal equivalent. Hint: To obtain octal equivalent of an integer, divide it continuously by 8 till dividend doesn't become zero, then write the remainders obtained in reverse direction.

*Program:*

```
/* Find octal equivalent of a number */
# include <stdio.h>
# include <math.h>
int main( )
{
    int n1, n2, rem, oct, p ;
    printf ( "\nEnter any number: " ) ;
    scanf ( "%d", &n1 ) ;
    n2 = n1 ;
    p = oct = 0 ;
    while ( n1 > 0 )
    {
        rem = n1 % 8 ;
        n1 = n1 / 8 ;
        oct = oct + rem * pow ( 10.0, p ) ;
        p++ ;
    }
    printf ( "The octal equivalent of %d is %d\n", n2, oct ) ;
    return 0 ;
}
```

(f) Write a program to find the range of a set of numbers. Range is the difference between the smallest and biggest number in the list.

*Program:*

```
/* Program to find the range of a set of numbers */
# include <stdio.h>

int main( )
{
    int n, no, flag, small, big, range ;
    flag = 0 ;
    printf ( "\nHow many numbers are there in a set? " ) ;
    scanf ( "%d", &n ) ;
    while ( n > 0 )
    {
        printf ( "\nEnter no: " ) ;
        scanf ( "%d", &no ) ;
        if ( flag == 0 )
        {
            small = big = no ;
            flag = 1 ;
        }
        else
        {
            if ( no > big )
                big = no ;
            if ( no < small )
                small = no ;
        }
        n-- ;
    }
    if ( small < 0 )
        range = small + big ;
    else
        range = big - small ;
    if ( range < 0 )
        range = range * -1 ;
    printf ( "\nThe range of given set of numbers is %d\n", range ) ;
    return 0 ;
}
```

# CHAPTER SIX

# More Complex Repetitions

**[A]** Answer the following questions:

(a) The **break** statement is used to exit from:

1. an **if** statement
2. a **for** loop
3. a program
4. the **main( )** function

*Answer:*

(2) a **for** loop

(b) A **do-while** loop is useful when we want that the statements within the loop must be executed:

1. Only Once
2. At least once
3. More than once
4. None of the above

*Answer:*

(2) At least once

(c) In what sequence the initialization, testing and execution of body is done in a **do-while** loop?

1. Initialization, execution of body, testing
2. Execution of body, initialization, testing
3. Initialization, testing, execution of body

4. None of the above

*Answer:*

1. Initialization, execution of body, testing

(d) Which of the following is not an infinite loop?

1.
```
int i = 1 ;
while ( 1 )
{
  i++ ;
}
```

2.
```
for ( ; ; ) ;
```

3.
```
int True = 0, false ;
while ( True )
{
  False = 1 ;
}
```

4.
```
int y, x = 0 ;
do
{
  y = x ;
} while ( x == 0 ) ;
```

*Answer:*

3

(e) Which of the following statements are true for the following program?

```
# include <stdio.h>
int main( )
{
    int x = 10, y = 100 % 90 ;
    for ( i = 1 ; i <= 10 ; i++ ) ;
        if ( x != y ) ;
            printf ( "x = %d y = %d\n", x, y ) ;
    return 0 ;
}
```

(1) The **printf( )** function is called 10 times.
(2) The program will produce the output x = 10 y = 10.
(3) The ; after the **if ( x != y )** will not produce an error.
(4) The program will not produce any output.
(5) The **printf( )** function is called infinite times.

*Answer:*

(2) The program will produce the output x = 10 y = 10.

(f) Which of the following statement is true about a **for** loop used in a C program?

(1) **for** loop works faster than a **while** loop.
(2) All things that can be done using a **for** loop can also be done using a **while** loop.
(3) **for ( ; ; )** implements an infinite loop.
(4) **for** loop can be used if we want statements in a loop to get executed at least once.
(5) **for** loop works faster than a **do-while** loop.

*Answer:*

(2), (3), (4).

**[B]** Attempt the following questions:

(a) Write a program to print the multiplication table of the number entered by the user. The table should get displayed in the following form:

29 * 1 = 29
29 * 2 = 58
...

*Program:*

```
/* Generate and print table of a given number */
# include <stdio.h>
int main( )
{
    int i, num ;
    printf ( "\nEnter the number: " ) ;
    scanf ( "%d", &num ) ;
    for ( i = 1 ; i <= 10 ; i++ )
        printf ( "%d * %d = %d\n", num, i, num * i ) ;
    return 0 ;
}
```

(b) According to a study, the approximate level of intelligence of a person can be calculated using the following formula:

i = 2 + ( y + 0.5 x )

Write a program that will produce a table of values of **i**, **y** and **x**, where **y** varies from 1 to 6, and, for each value of **y**, **x** varies from 5.5 to 12.5 in steps of 0.5.

*Program:*

```
/* Generate and print intelligence table */
# include <stdio.h>
int main( )
{
    int y ;
    float i, x ;
    for ( y = 1 ; y <= 6 ; y++ )
    {
        for ( x = 5.5 ; x <= 12.5 ; x += 0.5 )
        {
            i = 2 + ( y + 0.5 * x ) ;
            printf ( "y = %d, x = %f i = %f\n", y, x, i ) ;
        }
    }
    return 0 ;
}
```

(c) When interest compounds **q** times per year at an annual rate of **r** % for **n** years, the principal **p** compounds to an amount **a** as per the following formula

$a = p ( 1 + r / q )^{nq}$

Write a program to read 10 sets of **p**, **r**, **n** & **q** and calculate the corresponding **a**s.

*Program:*

```
/* Compound interest calculation */
# include <stdio.h>
# include <math.h>
int main( )
```

```
{
    float  q, r, n, p, a ;
    int  i ;
    for ( i = 1 ; i <= 10 ; i++ )
    {
        printf ( "\nEnter the principal amount:" ) ;
        scanf ( "%f", &p ) ;
        printf ( "\nEnter the rate of interest:" ) ;
        scanf ( "%f", &r ) ;
        printf ( "\nEnter the number of years: " ) ;
        scanf ( "%f", &n ) ;
        printf ( "\nEnter the compounding period: " ) ;
        scanf ( "%f", &q ) ;
        a = p + pow ( (1 + ( r / q ) ), ( n * q ) ) ;
        printf ( "\n\nTotal amount = %f\n", a ) ;
    }
    return 0 ;
}
```

(d) The natural logarithm can be approximated by the following series.

$$\frac{x-1}{x}+\frac{1}{2}\left(\frac{x-1}{x}\right)^2+\frac{1}{2}\left(\frac{x-1}{x}\right)^3+\frac{1}{2}\left(\frac{x-1}{x}\right)^4+\ldots.$$

If **x** is input through the keyboard, write a program to calculate the sum of first seven terms of this series.

*Program:*

```
/* Compute natural logarithm */
# include <stdio.h>
# include <math.h>
int main( )
{
    int  x, i ;
    float  result = 0 ;
    printf ( "\nEnter the value of x: " ) ;
    scanf ( "%d", &x ) ;
    for ( i = 1; i <= 7 ; i++ )
    {
        if ( i == 1 )
            result = result + pow ( ( x - 1.0 ) / x, i ) ;
```

```
        else
            result = result + ( 1.0 / 2 ) * pow ( ( x - 1.0 ) / x, i ) ;
    }
    printf ( "\nLog ( %d ) = %f\n", x, result ) ;
    return 0 ;
}
```

(e) Write a program to generate all Pythagorean Triplets with side length less than or equal to 30.

*Program:*

```
/* Generate Pythagorean Triplets */
#include <stdio.h>
int main( )
{
    int i, j, k ;
    for ( i = 1 ; i <= 30 ; i++ )
    {
        for ( j = 1 ; j <= 30 ; j++ )
        {
            for ( k = 1 ; k <= 30 ; k++ )
            {
                if ( i * i + j * j == k * k )
                    printf ( "%d %d %d\n", i, j, k ) ;
            }
        }
    }
    return 0 ;
}
```

(f) Population of a town today is 100000. The population has increased steadily at the rate of 10% per year for last 10 years. Write a program to determine the population at the end of each year in the last decade.

*Program:*

```
/* Determine population growth over last decade */
#include <stdio.h>
#include <math.h>
```

```
int main( )
{
    int pop, n ;
    float p, r ;
    r = 10 ;
    p = 100000 ;
    for ( n = 1 ; n <= 10 ; n++ )
    {
        pop = p / pow ( ( 1 + r / 100 ), n ) ;
        printf ( "Population %d years ago = %d\n", n, pop ) ;
    }
    return 0 ;
}
```

(g) Ramanujan number (1729) is the smallest number that can be expressed as sum of two cubes in two different ways—1729 can be expressed as $1^3 + 12^3$ and $9^3 + 10^3$. Write a program to print all such numbers up to a reasonable limit.

*Program:*

```
/* Generate Ramanujan numbers */
#include <stdio.h>
int main( )
{
    int i, j, k, l ;
    for ( i = 1 ; i <= 30 ; i++ )
    {
        for ( j = 1 ; j <= 30 ; j++ )
        {
            for ( k = 1 ; k <= 30 ; k++ )
            {
                for ( l = 1 ; l <= 30 ; l++ )
                {
                    if ( ( i != j && i != k && i != l ) &&
                         ( j != i && j != k && j != l ) &&
                         ( k != i && k != j && k != l ) &&
                         ( l != i && l != j && l != k ) )
                    {
                        if ( i * i * i + j * j * j == k * k * k + l * l * l )
                            printf ( "%d %d %d %d\n", i, j, k, l ) ;
```

```
                    }
                }
            }
        }
    }
    return 0 ;
}
```

(h) Write a program to print 24 hours of day with suitable suffixes like AM, PM, Noon and Midnight.

*Program:*

```
/* Print hours of the day with suitable suffixes */
#include <stdio.h>
int main( )
{
    int  hour ;
    for ( hour = 0 ; hour <= 23 ; hour++ )
    {
        if ( hour == 0 )
        {
            printf ( "12 Midnight\n" ) ;
            continue ;
        }
        if ( hour < 12 )
            printf ( "%d AM\n", hour ) ;
        if ( hour == 12 )
            printf ( "12 Noon\n" ) ;
        if ( hour > 12 )
            printf ( "%d PM\n", hour % 12 ) ;
    }
    return 0 ;
}
```

(i) Write a program to produce the following output:

```
            1
        2       3
    4       5       6
7       8       9       10
```

*Program:*

```
/* Produce the given pattern */
# include <stdio.h>
int main( )
{
    int i , j, k, l, sp ;
    sp = 20 ;
    for ( i = 1, k = 1 ; i < 5 ; i++ )
    {
        for ( l = 1 ; l <= sp ; l++ )
            printf ( " " ) ;
        sp -= 2 ;
        for ( j = 1 ; j <= i ; j++, k++ )
            printf ( " %d  ", k ) ;
        printf ( "\n" ) ;
    }
    return 0 ;
}
```

# CHAPTER SEVEN

# Case Control Instruction

**[A]** What will be the output of the following programs?

(a)
```
# include <stdio.h>
int main( )
{
    char  suite = 3 ;
    switch ( suite )
    {
        case 1 :
            printf ( "Diamond\n" ) ;
        case 2 :
            printf ( "Spade\n" ) ;
        default :
            printf ( "Heart\n" ) ;
    }
    printf ( "I thought one wears a suite\n" ) ;
    return 0 ;
}
```

*Output:*

Heart
I thought one wears a suite

(b)
```
# include <stdio.h>
int main( )
{
    int  c = 3 ;
    switch ( c )
    {
```

```
        case '3' :
            printf ( "You never win the silver prize\n" ) ;
            break ;
        case 3 :
            printf ( "You always lose the gold prize\n" ) ;
            break ;
        default :
            printf ( "Of course provided you win a prize\n" ) ;
    }
    return 0 ;
}
```

*Output:*

You always lose the gold prize

(c)
```
# include <stdio.h>
int main( )
{
    int  i = 3 ;
    switch ( i )
    {
        case 0 :
            printf ( "Customers are dicey\n" ) ;
        case 1 + 2 :
            printf ( "Markets are pricey\n" ) ;
        case 4 / 2 :
            printf ( "Investors are moody\n" ) ;
    }
    return 0 ;
}
```

*Output:*

Markets are pricey

(d)
```
# include <stdio.h>
int main( )
{
    int  k ;
    float j = 2.0 ;
    switch ( k = j + 1 )
    {
```

```
        case 3 :
            printf ( "Trapped\n" ) ;
            break ;
        default :
            printf ( "Caught!\n" ) ;
    }
    return 0 ;
}
```

*Output:*

Trapped

(e)
```
# include <stdio.h>
int main( )
{
    int  ch = 'a' + 'b' ;
    switch ( ch )
    {
        case 'a' :
        case 'b' :
            printf ( "Look at 10 ideas, 11th will occur to you\n" ) ;
        case 'A' :
            printf ( "If you have a good idea, project it\n" ) ;
        case 'b' + 'a' :
            printf ( "Have ideas, will fly\n" ) ;
    }
    return 0 ;
}
```

*Output:*

You entered a and b

**[B]** Point out the errors, if any, in the following programs:

(a)
```
# include <stdio.h>
int main( )
{
    int  suite = 1 ;
    switch ( suite ) ;
    {
        case 0 ;
            printf ( "Club\n" ) ;
```

```
        case 1 ;
            printf ( "Diamond\n" ) ;
    }
    return 0 ;
}
```

Error. Semi-colon after *switch* statement and after *case 0* and *case 1*.

(b)
```
# include <stdio.h>
int main( )
{
    int temp ;
    scanf ( "%d", &temp ) ;
    switch ( temp )
    {
        case ( temp <= 20 ) :
            printf ( "Ooooooohhhh! Damn cool! \n" ) ;
        case ( temp > 20 && temp <= 30 ) :
            printf ( "Rain rain here again! \n" ) ;
        case ( temp > 30 && temp <= 40 ) :
            printf ( "Wish I am on Everest\n" ) ;
        default :
            printf ( "Good old Nagpur weather\n" ) ;
    }
    return 0 ;
}
```

Error. Relational operators cannot be used in cases.

(c)
```
# include <stdio.h>
int main( )
{
    float a = 3.5 ;
    switch ( a )
    {
        case 0.5 :
            printf ( "The art of C\ " ) ;
            break ;
        case 1.5 :
```

```
            printf ( "The spirit of C\n" ) ;
            break ;
        case 2.5 :
            printf ( "See through C\n" ) ;
            break ;
    }
    return 0 ;
}
```

Error. Floats cannot be used in cases.

(d)
```
# include <stdio.h>
int main( )
{
    int a = 3, b = 4, c ;
    c = b – a ;
    switch ( c )
    {
        case 1 || 2 :
            printf ( "God give me a chance to change things\n" ) ;
            break ;
        case a || b :
            printf ( "God give me  chance to run my show\n" ) ;

            break ;
    }
    return 0 ;
}
```

Error. A case needs a constant expression. Logical operators cannot be used in cases.

**[C]** Write a program which to find the grace marks for a student using **switch**. The user should enter the class obtained by the student and the number of subjects he has failed in. Use the following logic:

- If the student gets first class and he fails in more than 3 subjects, he does not get any grace. Otherwise, he gets a grace of 5 marks per subject.

- If the student gets second class and he fails in more than 2 subjects, he does not get any grace. Otherwise, he gets a grace of 4 marks per subject.

- If the student gets third class and he fails in more than 1 subject, then he does not get any grace. Otherwise, he gets a grace of 5 marks.

*Program:*

```
/* Determine the grace marks obtained by student */
# include <stdio.h>

int main( )
{
    int  c, sub ;

    printf ( "\nEnter the class and number of subjects failed: " ) ;
    scanf ( "%d %d", &c, &sub ) ;

    switch ( c )
    {
        case 1 :
            if ( sub <= 3 )
                printf ( "Student gets total of %d grace marks\n",
                         5 * sub ) ;
            else
                printf ( "No grace marks\n" ) ;
            break ;

        case 2 :
            if ( sub <= 2 )
                printf ( "Student gets total of %d grace marks\n",
                         4 * sub ) ;
            else
                printf ( "No grace marks\n" ) ;
            break ;

        case 3 :
            if ( sub == 1 )
                printf ( "Student gets 5 grace marks\n" ) ;
            else
```

```
            printf ( "No grace marks\n" ) ;
        break ;

    default :
        printf ( "Wrong class entered\n" ) ;
}

return 0 ;
}
```

# CHAPTER EIGHT

# Functions

**[A]** Point out the errors, if any, in the following programs:

(a)
```
# include <stdio.h>
int addmult ( int, int )
int main( )
{
    int i = 3, j = 4, k, l ;
    k = addmult ( i, j ) ;
    l = addmult ( i, j ) ;
    printf ( "%d %d\n", k, l ) ;
    return 0 ;
}
int addmult ( int x, int y )
{
    int u, v ;
    u = x + y ;
    v = x * y ;
    return ( u, v ) ;
}
```

Error. Missing ; in prototype declaration of **addmult( )**. Also, a function cannot return 2 values at a time.

(b)
```
# include <stdio.h>
int main( )
{
    int a ;
    a = message( ) ;
    return 0 ;
}
void message( )
```

```
{
    printf ( "Learn from him online at ykanetkar.com\n" ) ;
    return ;
}
```

Error. Prototype of **message( )** is missing.

(c)
```
# include <stdio.h>
int main( )
{
    float a = 15.5 ;
    char ch = 'C' ;
    printit ( a, ch ) ;
    return 0 ;
}
printit ( a, ch )
{
    printf ( "%f %c\n", a, ch ) ;
}
```

Error. **a** and **ch** should be declared as **float** and **char** respectively in the function **printit( )**.

(d)
```
# include <stdio.h>
int main( )
{
    let_us_c( )
    {
        printf ( "Learn C online...\n" ) ;
        printf ( "At ykanetkar.com\n" ) ;
    }
    return 0 ;
}
```

Error. One function cannot be defined within another function.

**[B]** State whether the following statements are True or False:

(a) Commonly used variables are available to all the functions in a program.

Answer: False

(b) To return the control back to the calling function we must use the keyword **return**.

Answer: False

(c) The same variable names can be used in different functions without any conflict.

Answer: True

(d) Every called function must contain a **return** statement.

Answer: False

(e) A function may contain more than one **return** statement.

Answer: True

(f) Each **return** statement in a function may return a different value.

Answer: True

(g) A function can still be useful even if you don't pass any arguments to it and the function doesn't return any value.

Answer: True

(h) Same names can be used for different functions without any conflict.

Answer: False

(i) A function may be called more than once from any other function.

Answer: True

**[C]** Answer the following questions:

(a) Any year is entered through the keyboard. Write a function to determine whether the year is a leap year or not.

*Program:*

```
/* Using a function, determine whether a year is leap year or not */
# include <stdio.h>
void leapyear ( int ) ;
int main( )
{
```

```
    int  year ;
    printf ( "\nEnter year: " ) ;
    scanf ( "%d", &year ) ;
    leapyear ( year ) ;  /* Function call */
    return 0 ;
}
void leapyear ( int year )
{
    if ( year % 4 == 0 && year % 100 != 0 || year % 400 == 0 )
        printf ( "%d is leap year\n", year ) ;
    else
        printf ( "%d is not a leap year\n", year ) ;
}
```

(b) A positive integer is entered through the keyboard. Write a function to obtain the prime factors of this number.

For example, prime factors of 24 are 2, 2, 2 and 3, whereas prime factors of 35 are 5 and 7.

*Program:*

```
/* Obtain prime factors of a number */
# include <stdio.h>
void prime ( int ) ;
int main( )
{
    int  num ;
    printf ( "Enter number:" ) ;
    scanf ( "%d", &num ) ;
    prime ( num ) ;  /* Function call */
    return 0 ;
}
void prime ( int num )
{
    int  i = 2 ;
    printf ( "Prime factors of %d are ", num ) ;
    while ( num != 1 )
    {
        if ( num % i == 0 )
            printf ( "%d ", i ) ;
        else
```

```
            {
                i++ ;
                continue ;
            }
            num = num / i ;
        }
    }
```

# CHAPTER NINE

# Pointers

**[A]** What will be the output of the following programs?

(a)
```
# include <stdio.h>
void fun ( int, int ) ;
int main( )
{
    int i = 5, j = 2 ;
    fun ( i, j ) ;
    printf ( "%d %d\n", i, j ) ;
    return 0 ;
}
void fun ( int i, int j )
{
    i = i * i ;
    j = j * j ;
}
```

*Output:*

```
5 2
```

(b)
```
# include <stdio.h>
void fun ( int *, int * ) ;
int main( )
{
    int i = 5, j = 2 ;
    fun ( &i, &j ) ;
    printf ( "%d %d\n", i, j ) ;
    return 0 ;
}
void fun ( int *i, int *j )
{
```

```
    *i = *i * *i ;
    *j = *j * *j ;
}
```

*Output:*

25 4

(c)
```
# include <stdio.h>
int main( )
{
    float a = 13.5 ;
    float *b, *c ;
    b = &a ; /* suppose address of a is 1006 */
    c = b ;
    printf ( "%u %u %u\n", &a, b, c ) ;
    printf ( "%f %f %f %f %f\n", a, *(&a), *&a, *b, *c ) ;
    return 0 ;
}
```

*Output:*

1006 1006 1006
13.500000 13.500000 13.500000 13.500000 13.500000
Note : Instead of 1006 you may get some other address

**[B]** Point out the errors, if any, in the following programs:

(a)
```
# include <stdio.h>
int main( )
{
    float p = 23.24 ;
    int *q, **r ;
    q = &p ;
    r = &q ;
    printf ( "%f %f\n", *q, **r ) ;
    return 0 ;
}
```

Error. **q** should be declared as **float** pointer and **r** should be declared as pointer to float pointer.

(b)
```
# include <stdio.h>
int main( )
```

```
{
    char ch = 'A' ;
    int k = 35 ;
    float a = 3.14 ;
    printf ( "%p %p %p\n", &ch, &k, &a ) ;
    return 0 ;
}
```

No Error.

(c)
```
# include <stdio.h>
void function ( int * ) ;
int main( )
{
    int i = 35, *z ;
    z = function ( &i ) ;
    printf ( "%d\n", z ) ;
    return 0 ;
}
void function ( int *m )
{
    return ( m + 2 ) ;
}
```

Error. Not an allowed type.

**[C]** Attempt the following questions:

(a) Given three variables **x, y, z** write a function to circularly shift their values to right. In other words, if x = 5, y = 8, z = 10, after circular shift y = 5, z = 8, x =10. Call the function with variables **a, b, c** to circularly shift values.

*Program:*

```
/* Circular shifting of values */
# include <stdio.h>
void fun ( int, int, int ) ;
int main( )
{
    int x, y, z ;
    printf ( "Enter the values x, y, z:\n" ) ;
```

```
    scanf ( "%d%d%d", &x, &y, &z ) ;
    printf ( "\nValues of x, y & z as entered:" ) ;
    printf ( "\nx = %d\ty = %d\tz = %d\n", x, y, z ) ;
    fun ( x, y, z ) ;
    return 0 ;
}
/* Function to shift values of x, y & z */
void fun ( int x, int y, int z )
{
    int i, t ;
    for ( i = 0 ; i <= 2 ; i++ )
    {
        t = z ;
        z = y ;
        y = x ;
        x = t ;
        printf ( "\nAfter right shifting %d time(s):\n", i + 1 ) ;
        printf ( "x = %d\ty = %d\tz = %d", x, y, z ) ;
    }
}
```

(b) Define a function that receives weight of a commodity in Kilograms and returns the equivalent weight in Grams, Tons and Pounds. Call this function from **main( )** and print the results in **main( )**.

*Program:*

```
/* Weight conversion program */
# include <stdio.h>
void convert ( float, float *, float *, float * ) ;
int main( )
{
    float  kg, gm, ton, pound ;
    printf ( "\nEnter weight in Kilograms: " ) ;
    scanf ( "%f", &kg ) ;
    convert ( kg, &gm, &ton, &pound ) ;
    printf ( "Kg = %f\n ", kg ) ;
    printf ( "Gm = %f Tonne = %f Pounds = %f\n", gm, ton, pound ) ;
    return 0 ;
}
void convert ( float  kg, float *g, float *t, float *p )
```

```
{
    *g = kg * 1000 ;
    *t = kg * 0.001 ;
    *p = kg * 2.204 ;
}
```

(c) Define a function to compute the distance between two points and use it to develop another function that will compute the area of the triangle whose vertices are **A(x1, y1)**, **B(x2, y2)**, and **C(x3, y3)**. Use these functions to develop a function which returns a value 1 if the point **(x, y)** lines inside the triangle ABC, otherwise returns a value 0. Would you get any advantage if you develop these functions to work on call be reference principle?

*Program:*

```
/* Calculate distance between two points and use the function
   to calculate area of triangle given its three vertices */
# include <stdio.h>
# include <math.h>

float distance ( int  x1, int  y1, int  x2, int  y2 ) ;
float area( ) ;
int main( )
{
    int x1, x2, y1, y2 ;
    float  z, x ;
    printf ( "\nEnter the co-ordinates of two points: " ) ;
    scanf ( "%d%d%d%d", &x1, &y1, &x2, &y2 ) ;
    z = distance ( x1, y1, x2, y2 ) ;
    printf ( "\nDistance between Two points = %f\n", z ) ;
    x = area( ) ;
    printf ( "\nArea of the triangle = %f\n", x ) ;
    return 0 ;
}
/* Function to calculate distance */
float  distance ( int x1, int y1, int x2, int y2 )
{
    float m, d ;
    m = pow ( ( x2 - x1 ), 2 ) + pow ( ( y2 - y1 ), 2 ) ;
    d = sqrt ( m ) ;
```

```
    return d ;
}
/* Get vertices of triangle */
float area( )
{
    float triarea ( float, float, float ) ;
    float a, b, c, d ;
    int x1, x2, x3, x4, y1, y2, y3, y4 ;
    float area1, area2, area3, totarea ;
    float a1, b1, c1 ;
    printf ( "\nEnter the co-ordinates of three points: " ) ;
    scanf ( "%d%d%d%d%d%d", &x1, &y1, &x2, &y2, &x3, &y3 ) ;
    printf ( "\nEnter the co-ordinates of one more point: " ) ;
    scanf ( "%d%d", &x4, &y4 ) ;
    a = distance ( x1, y1, x2, y2 ) ;
    b = distance ( x1, y1, x3, y3 ) ;
    c = distance ( x2, y2, x3, y3 ) ;
    d = triarea ( a, b, c ) ;
    a1 = distance ( x1, y1, x4, y4 ) ;
    b1 = distance ( x2, y2, x4, y4 ) ;
    c1 = distance ( x3, y3, x4, y4 ) ;
    area1 = triarea ( a, a1, b1 ) ;
    area2 = triarea ( b, a1, c1 ) ;
    area3 = triarea ( c, b1, c1 ) ;
    totarea = area1 + area2 + area3 ;
    if ( ( totarea - d ) <= 0.0009 )
        printf ( "\nPoint  ( %d, %d ) is inside Triangle\n", x4, y4 ) ;
    else
        printf ( "\nPoint  ( %d, %d ) lies outside Triangle\n", x4, y4 ) ;
    return d ;
}
/* Function to calculate area from a formula */
float triarea ( float a, float b, float c )
{
    float s, m, x ;
    s = ( a + b + c ) / 2 ;
    m = s * ( s - a ) * ( s - b ) * ( s - c ) ;
    x = sqrt ( m ) ;
    return ( x ) ;
}
```

There is no distinct advantage in using a call by reference principle since **distance( ), area( )** and **triarea( )** all are returning only one value when called.

# CHAPTER
# Ten

# Recursion

**[A]** What will be the output of the following programs?

(a)
```
# include <stdio.h>
int main( )
{
    printf ( "I C, you C, we all C\n" ) ;
    main( ) ;
    return 0 ;
}
```

*Output:*

The message will get printed indefinitely.

(b)
```
# include <stdio.h>
# include <stdlib.h>
int main( )
{
    int i = 0 ;
    i++ ;
    if ( i <= 5 )
    {
        printf ( "C adds wings to your thoughts\n" ) ;
        exit ( 0 ) ;
        main( ) ;
    }
    return 0 ;
}
```

*Output:*

C adds wings to your thoughts

**[B]** Attempt the following questions:

(a) A positive integer is entered through the keyboard, write a function to find the binary equivalent of this number:

(1) Without using recursion
(2) Using recursion

*Program:*

```
/* Binary equivalent of a decimal number */
# include <stdio.h>
int binary ( int  ) ;
int main( )
{
    int  num ;
    printf ( "\nEnter the number: " ) ;
    scanf ( "%d", &num ) ;
    binary ( num ) ;  /* Function call */
    return 0 ;
}
/* function to convert decimal to binary */
int binary ( int  n )
{
    int  r ;
    r = n % 2 ;
    n = n / 2 ;
    if ( n == 0 )
    {
        printf ( "\nThe binary equivalent is %d", r ) ;
        return ( r ) ;
    }
    else
        binary ( n ) ;     /* Recursive call */
    printf ( "%d", r ) ;
}
```

(b) Write a recursive function to obtain the running sum of first 25 natural numbers.

*Program:*

```
/* Program to obtain running sum of natural numbers */
# include <stdio.h>
int getsum ( int ) ;
int main( )
{
    int s ;
    s = getsum ( 0 ) ;
    printf ( "The sum of first 25 natural numbers is %d\n", s ) ;
    return 0 ;
}
int getsum ( int n )
{
    int sum = 0 ;
    if ( n == 25 )
        return sum ;
    sum = n + getsum ( ++n ) ;
    return ( sum ) ;
}
```

(c) There are three pegs labeled A, B and C. Four disks are placed on peg A. The bottom-most disk is largest, and disks go on decreasing in size with the topmost disk being smallest. The objective of the game is to move the disks from peg A to peg C, using peg B as an auxiliary peg. The rules of the game are as follows:

(1) Only one disk may be moved at a time, and it must be the top disk on one of the pegs.

(2) A larger disk should never be placed on the top of a smaller disk.

Write a program to print out the sequence in which the disks should be moved such that all disks on peg A are finally transferred to peg C.

*Program:*

```
#include <stdio.h>
void move ( int, char, char, char ) ;
int main( )
{
```

```
    int n = 4 ;
    move ( n, 'A', 'B', 'C' ) ;
    return 0 ;
}
void move ( int n, char sp, char ap, char ep )
{
    if ( n == 1 )
        printf ( "Move from %c to %c\n", sp, ep ) ;
    else
    {
        move ( n - 1, sp, ep, ap ) ;
        move ( 1, sp,' ', ep ) ;
        move ( n - 1, ap, sp, ep ) ;
    }
}
```

# CHAPTER

# ELEVEN

# Data Types Revisited

**[A]** What will be the output of the following programs?

(a)
```
# include <stdio.h>
int  i = 0 ;
void val( ) ;
int main( )
{
    printf ( "main's i = %d\n", i ) ;
    i++ ;
    val( ) ;
    printf ( "main's i = %d\n", i ) ;
    val( ) ;
    return 0 ;
}
void val( )
{
    i = 100 ;
    printf ( "val's i = %d\n", i ) ;
    i++ ;
}
```

*Output:*

```
main's i = 0
val's i = 100
main's i = 101
val's i = 100
```

(b)
```
# include <stdio.h>
int main( )
{
    static int  count = 5 ;
    printf ( "count = %d\n", count-- ) ;
    if ( count != 0 )
        main( ) ;
    return 0 ;
}
```

*Output:*

```
count = 5
count = 4
count = 3
count = 2
count = 1
```

(c)
```
# include <stdio.h>
void func( ) ;
int main( )
{
    func( ) ;  func( ) ;
    return 0 ;
}
void func( )
{
    auto int  i = 0 ;
    register int j = 0 ;
    static int k = 0 ;
    i++ ;  j++ ;  k++ ;
    printf ( "%d %d %d\n", i, j, k ) ;
}
```

*Output:*

```
1 1 1
1 1 2
```

(d)
```
# include <stdio.h>
int x = 10 ;
int main( )
{
    int x = 20 ;
```

```
    {
        int x = 30 ;
        printf ( "%d\n", x ) ;
    }
    printf ( "%d\n", x ) ;
    return 0 ;
}
```

*Output:*

```
30
20
```

**[B]** Point out the errors, if any, in the following programs:

(a)
```
# include <stdio.h>
int main( )
{
    long num ;
    num = 2 ;
    printf ( "%d\n", num ) ;
    return 0 ;
}
```

No Error

(b)
```
# include <stdio.h>
int main( )
{
    char ch = 200 ;
    printf ( "%d\n", ch ) ;
    return 0 ;
}
```

No Error

(c)
```
# include <stdio.h>
int main( )
{
    unsigned a = 25 ; long unsigned b = 25l ;
    printf ( "%lu %u\n", a, b ) ;
    return 0 ;
}
```

Error. Format %lu should be used for b and %u should be used for a.

(d)
```
# include <stdio.h>
int main( )
{
    long float a = 25.345e454 ;  unsigned double b = 25 ;
    printf ( "%lf %d\n", a, b ) ;
    return 0 ;
}
```

Error. Format %lf should be used for b.

**[C]** State whether the following statements are True or False:

(a) The value of an automatic storage class variable persists between various function invocations.

*Answer: False*

(b) If the CPU registers are not available, the register storage class variables are treated as static storage class variables.

*Answer: False*

(c) If we try to use register storage class for a **float** variable the compiler will report an error message.

*Answer: False*

(d) The default value for automatic variable is zero.

*Answer: False*

(e) The life of static variable is till the control remains within the block in which it is defined.

*Answer: False*

(f) If a global variable is to be defined, then the **extern** keyword is necessary in its declaration.

*Answer: False*

(g) The address of register variable is not accessible.

*Answer: True*

# CHAPTER

# TWELVE

# The C Preprocessor

**[A]** Answer the following questions:

(a) A preprocessor directive is:

1. a message from compiler to the programmer
2. a message from compiler to the linker
3. a message from programmer to the preprocessor
4. a message from programmer to the microprocessor

*Answer:*

(3) a message from programmer to the preprocessor

(b) Which of the following are correctly formed **#define** statements?

```
#define  INCH PER FEET  12
#define  SQR (X)  ( X * X )
#define  SQR(X)  X * X
#define  SQR(X)  ( X * X )
```

*Answer:*

```
#define SQR(X) ( X * X )
```

(c) State True or False:

(1) A macro must always be written in capital letters.

Answer: False

(2) A macro must always be accommodated in a single line.

Answer: Usually true. Some compilers allow multi-line macros

(3) After preprocessing when the program is sent for compilation the macros are removed from the expanded source code.

Answer: True

(4) Macros with arguments are not allowed.

Answer: False

(5) Nested macros are allowed.

Answer: False

(6) In a macro call the control is passed to the macro.

Answer: False

(d) A header file is:

1. A file that contains standard library functions
2. A file that contains function declarations and macros
3. A file that contains user-defined functions
4. A file that is present in current working directory

*Answer:*

2. A file that contains definitions and macros

(e) All macro substitutions in a program are done

1. Before compilation of the program
2. After compilation of the program
3. During execution of the program
4. During linking of the program

*Answer:*

1. Before compilation of the program

**[B]** What will be the output of the following programs?

(a) # include <stdio.h>

```
int main( )
{
    int i = 2 ;
    # ifdef DEF
        i *= i ;
    # else
        printf ( "%d\n", i ) ;
    # endif
    return 0 ;
}
```

*Output:*

2

(b)
```
# include <stdio.h>
# define PRODUCT(x) ( x * x )
int main( )
{
    int  i = 3, j, k, l ;
    j = PRODUCT( i + 1 ) ;
    k = PRODUCT( i++ ) ;
    l = PRODUCT ( ++i ) ;
    printf ( "%d %d %d %d\n", i, j, k, l ) ;
    return 0 ;
}
```

*Output:*

7 7 9 49

(c)
```
# include <stdio.h>
# define PI  3.14
# define AREA( x, y, z )   ( PI * x * x + y * z ) ;

int main( )
{
    float a = AREA ( 1, 5, 8 ) ;
    float b = AREA ( AREA ( 1, 5, 8 ), 4, 5 ) ;
    printf ( " a = %f\n", a ) ;
    printf ( " b = %f\n", b ) ;
    return 0 ;
}
```

*Output:*

Error. Since there is a semicolon in the macro definition of **AREA**. If we drop the semicolon then the program will compile successfully. Nested macros are allowed.

**[C]** Attempt the following questions:

(a) If a macro is not getting expanded as per your expectation, how will you find out how is it being expanded by the preprocessor.

*Answer:*

In such a case we should preprocess our program and see the expanded source code. Assuming that you program is stored in a file called PR1.C, For Turbo C++ environment this can be done as shown below:

```
C:\> CPP PR1.C
```

Here CPP stands for C PreProcessor. On running this preprocessor on PR1.C a file PR1.I will get created. This file contains the expanded source code. This file can be opened in Turbo C++ editor (or any other editor) and its contents can be viewed to find out how the macro has been expanded by the preprocessor.

(b) Write macro definitions for the following:

1. To find arithmetic mean of two numbers.
2. To find absolute value of a number.
3. To convert an uppercase alphabet to lowercase.
4. To obtain the bigger of two numbers.

*Program:*

```
# include <stdio.h>
/* Macros Defined Below */
#define MEAN(x,y) ( ( x + y ) / 2 )
#define ABS(x) ( x < 0 ? x * - 1 : x )
#define TOLOWER(x) ( x + 32 )
#define BIG(x,y,z) ( x > y && x > z ? x : y > x && y > z ? y : z )
int main( )
{
    char ch ;
```

```
    int d, a, b, c ;
    printf ( "\nEnter any two numbers: " ) ;
    scanf ( "%d %d", &a, &b ) ;
    d = MEAN ( a, b ) ; /* Macro substitution */
    printf ( "Mean is %d\n", d ) ;
    printf ( "\nEnter any number: " ) ;
    scanf ( "%d", &a ) ;
    d = ABS ( a ) ;
    printf ( "Absolute value is %d\n", d ) ;
    fflush ( stdin ) ;
    printf ( "\nEnter any upper case character: " ) ;
    scanf ( "%c", &ch ) ;
    ch = TOLOWER ( ch ) ;
    printf ( "Lower case character is %c\n", ch ) ;
    printf ( "\nEnter any three numbers: " ) ;
    scanf ( "%d %d %d", &a, &b, &c ) ;
    d = BIG ( a, b, c ) ;
    printf ( "Big number is: %d\n", d ) ;
    return 0 ;
}
```

(c) Write macro definitions with arguments for calculation of Simple Interest and Amount. Store these macro definitions in a file "interest.h". Include this file in your program, and use the macro definitions for calculating Simple Interest and Amount.

*Program:*

```
/* interest.h */

/* Storing the macro definitions of Simple Interest and Amount in
the "interest.h" header file */
#define SI( p, n, r ) ( p * n * r / 100 )
#define AMT( p, SI ) ( p + SI )


/* Main Program to calculate simple interest and amount by
including "interest.h" header file*/
# include <stdio.h>
# include "interest.h"
int main( )
{
```

```
    int p, n ;
    float si, amt, r ;
    printf ( "\nEnter Principal, no. of years and rate of interest: " ) ;
    scanf ( "%d %d %f", &p, &n, &r ) ;
    si = SI ( p, n, r ) ;
    amt = AMT ( si, p ) ;
    printf ( "Simple interest is: %f\nAmount is: %f\n", si, amt ) ;

    return 0 ;
}
```

# CHAPTER

# THIRTEEN

# Arrays

**[A]** Answer the following questions:

(a) Are the following array declarations correct?

```
int  a (25) ;
int size = 10, b[ size ] ;
```

*Answer:*

No. All the declarations are wrong.

(b) Which element of the array does this expression reference?

```
num[ 4 ]
```

*Answer:*

Fifth element.

(c) What is the difference between the 5's in these two expressions? (Select the correct answer)

```
int  num[ 5 ] ;
num[ 5 ] = 11 ;
```

*Answer:*

First 5 is array size, second 5 refers to the $5^{th}$ element in the array.

(d) What will happen if you try to put so many values into an array when you initialize it that the size of the array is exceeded?

*Answer:*

Possible system malfunction

(e) What will happen if you put too few elements in an array when you initialize it?

*Answer:*

Unused elements will be filled with 0's or garbage

(f) What will happen if you assign a value to an element of an array whose subscript exceeds the size of the array?

*Answer:*

Other data may be overwritten

(g) When you pass an array as an argument to a function, what actually gets passed?

*Answer:*

Address of the array

(h) If you don't initialize a static array, what will its elements be set to?

*Answer:*

0

(i) if **int s[ 5 ]** is a one-dimensional array of integers, which of the following refers to the third element in the array using pointer notation?

*Answer:*

1. * ( s + 2 )

**[B]** Attempt the following questions:

(a) Twenty-five numbers are entered from the keyboard into an array. Write a program to find out how many of them are positive, how many are negative, how many are even and how many odd.

*Program*

```
/* Program to count positive, negative, odds & evens in an array */
# include <stdio.h>
int main( )
{
    int  num[ 25 ], i, neg = 0, pos = 0, odd = 0, even = 0 ;
    printf ( "Enter 25 elements of array" ) ;
    for ( i = 0 ; i <= 24 ; i++ )
        scanf ( "%d", &num[ i ] ) ;  /* Array Elements */
    for ( i = 0 ; i <= 24 ; i++ )
    {
        num[ i ] < 0 ? neg++ : ( pos++ ) ;  /* conditional operators */
        num[ i ] % 2 ? odd++ : ( even++ ) ;
    }
    printf ( "Negative elements = %d\n", neg ) ;
    printf ( "Positive elements = %d\n", pos ) ;
    printf ( "Even elements = %d\n", even ) ;
    printf ( "Odd elements = %d\n", odd ) ;
    return 0 ;
}
```

(b) If an array **arr** contains **n** elements, then write a program to check if **arr[ 0 ] = arr[ n - 1 ]**, **arr[ 1 ] = arr[ n - 2 ]** and so on.

*Program:*

```
/* Program to check if arr[ 0 ] = arr[ n - 1 ] and so on */
# include <stdio.h>
int main( )
{
    int arr[ 10 ], i, j ;
    printf ( "\nEnter 10 elements of array:\n" ) ;
    for ( i = 0 ; i <= 9 ; i++ )
        scanf ( "%d", &arr[ i ] ) ;
    for ( i = 0 ; i <= 4 ; i++ )
```

```
    {
        printf ( "arr[%d] and arr[%d] are ", i, 10 - ( i + 1 )) ;
        if ( arr[ i ] == arr[ 10 - ( i + 1 ) ] )
            printf ( "equal\n" ) ;
        else
            printf ( "unequal\n" ) ;
    }
    return 0 ;
}
```

(c) Write a program using pointers to find the smallest number in an array of 25 integers.

*Program:*

```
/* Program to find smallest element using pointer */
# include <stdio.h>
int main( )
{
    int arr[ 25 ], i, n ;
    printf ( "\nEnter 25 elements of array:\n" ) ;
    for ( i = 0 ; i <= 24 ; i++ )
        scanf ( "%d", &arr[ i ] ) ;
    n = *arr ;
    for ( i = 0 ; i <= 24 ; i++ )
    {
        if ( * ( arr + i ) < n )
            n = * ( arr + i ) ;
    }
    printf ( "Smallest number in array is %d\n", n ) ;
    return 0 ;
}
```

(d) Implement the Insertion sort algorithms shown in Figure 13.3 on a set of 25 numbers.

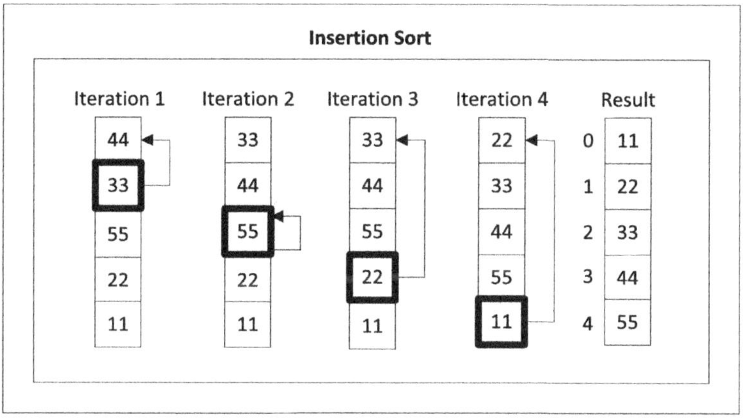


*Program*

```
/* Insertion Sort */
# include <stdio.h>
int main( )
{
    int  a[ 25 ], i, j, k, t ;
    printf ( "\nEnter 25 Numbers:\n" ) ;
    for ( i = 0 ; i <= 24 ; i++ )
        scanf ( "%d", &a[ i ] ) ;
    for ( i = 1 ; i <= 24 ; i++ )  /* number of passes */
    {

        t = a[ i ] ;
        for ( j = 0 ; j < i ; j++ )
        {
            if ( t < a[ j ] )
            {
                for ( k = i ; k >= j ; k-- )
                    a[ k ] = a[ k - 1 ] ;  /* shift elements to left */
                a[ j ] = t ;
                break ;
            }
        }
    }
    printf ( "\nSorted Numbers are:\n" ) ;
    for ( i = 0 ; i <= 24 ; i++ )
        printf ( "%d\n", a[ i ] ) ;
    return 0 ;
```

```
}
```

(e) Write a program which performs the following tasks:

- initialize an integer array of 10 elements in **main( )**
- pass the entire array to a function **modify( )**
- in **modify( )** multiply each element of array by 3
- return the control to **main( )** and print the new array elements in **main( )**

*Program:*

```
/* Program to pass the entire array & multiply each element by 3 */
# include <stdio.h>
void modify ( int *arr, int n ) ;
int main( )
{
    int i ;
    static int array[ ] = { 1, 2, 3, 4, 5, 6, 7, 8, 9, 10 } ;
    printf ( "\nOriginal Array is:\n" ) ;
    for ( i = 0 ; i < 10 ; i++ )
        printf ( "%d ", array[ i ] ) ;
    modify ( array, 10 ) ;
    printf ( "\n\nModified Array is: \n" ) ;
    for ( i = 0 ; i < 10 ; i++ )
        printf ( "%d ", array[ i ] ) ;
    return 0 ;
}
void modify ( int *arr, int n )
{
    int i ;
    for ( i = 0 ; i < n ; i++ )
    {
        *arr = *arr * 3 ;
        arr++ ;
    }
}
```

(f) For the following set of sample data, compute the standard deviation and the mean.

-6, -12, 8, 13, 11, 6, 7, 2, -6, -9, -10, 11, 10, 9, 2

The formula for standard deviation is

$$\frac{\sqrt{(x_i - \bar{x})^2}}{n}$$

where $\mathbf{x_i}$ is the data item and $\bar{\mathbf{x}}$ is the mean.

*Program:*

```
/* Computation of standard deviation */
# include <stdio.h>
# include <math.h>
int main( )
{
    int data[ ] = { -6, -12, 8, 13, 11, 6, 7, 2, -6, -9, 2, 11, 10, 9, -10 } ;
    float sum, xi, std, mean = 0 ;
    int i, n = 15 ;
    sum = 0 ;
    for ( i = 0 ; i <= 14 ; i++ )
        sum = sum + data[ i ] ;
    mean = sum / n ;
    /* Calculate standard deviation */
    sum = 0 ;
    for ( i = 0 ; i <= 14 ; i++ )
        sum = sum + pow ( ( data[ i ] - mean ), 2 ) ;
    std = sqrt ( sum ) / n ;
    for ( i = 0 ; i <= 14 ; i++ )
        printf ( "%d\t", data[ i ] ) ;
    printf ( "\nMean = %f\n", mean ) ;
    printf ( "Standard Deviation = %f\n", std ) ;
    return 0 ;
}
```

(g) The area of a triangle can be computed by the sine law when 2 sides of the triangle and the angle between them are known.

Area = (1 / 2 ) ab sin ( angle )

Given the following 6 triangular pieces of land, write a program to find their area and determine which is largest.

| Plot No. | a | b | angle |
|---|---|---|---|
| 1 | 137.4 | 80.9 | 0.78 |
| 2 | 155.2 | 92.62 | 0.89 |
| 3 | 149.3 | 97.93 | 1.35 |
| 4 | 160.0 | 100.25 | 9.00 |
| 5 | 155.6 | 68.95 | 1.25 |
| 6 | 149.7 | 120.0 | 1.75 |

*Program:*

```
/* Calculate Area = ( 1 / 2 ) ab sin ( angle ) */
# include <stdio.h>
# include <math.h>
int main( )
{
    float  t, a[ 6 ], b[ 6 ], angle[ 6 ], area[ 6 ], largest = 0.0 ;
    int  i, plot ;
    for ( i = 0 ; i <= 5 ; i++ )
    {
        printf ( "\nEnter the values of the following data:" ) ;
        printf ( "\na%d = ", i + 1 ) ;
        scanf ( "%f", &a[ i ] ) ;
        printf ( "\nb%d = ", i + 1 ) ;
        scanf ( "%f", &b[ i ] ) ;
        printf ( "\nangle%d = ", i + 1 ) ;
        scanf ( "%f", &angle[ i ] ) ;
        /* Calculate area */
        area[ i ] = ( 1.0 / 2 ) * a[ i ] * b[ i ] * sin ( angle[ i ] ) ;
        /* Note the largest value of area */
        if ( area[ i ] > largest )
        {
            largest = area[ i ] ;
            plot = i ;  /* note the element with largest area */
        }
    }
    /* Print area of all plots */
    printf ( "\n\nEntered Plot dimensions and Area is:\n" ) ;
    printf ( "\nPlot No.\ta\tb\tAngle\tArea" ) ;
```

```
    for ( i = 0 ; i <= 5 ; i++ )
    {
        printf ( "\n%d\t\t%.2f\t%.2f\t%.2f\t%.3f ", i+1, a[ i ], b[ i ],
                angle[ i ], area[ i ] ) ;
    }
    printf ( "\n\nLargest Triangular Area = %.3f:", largest ) ;
    printf ( "\n\na = %.2f\tb = %.2f\tangle = %.2f ", a[ plot ], b[ plot ],
            angle[ plot ] ) ;
    return 0 ;
}
```

(h) For the following set of n data points (x, y), compute the correlation coefficient r, given by

$$r = \frac{\sum xy - \sum x \sum y}{\sqrt{[n\sum x^2 - (\sum x)^2][n\sum y^2 - (\sum y)^2]}}$$

| x | y |
|---|---|
| 34.22 | 102.43 |
| 39.87 | 100.93 |
| 41.85 | 97.43 |
| 43.23 | 97.81 |
| 40.06 | 98.32 |
| 53.29 | 98.32 |
| 53.29 | 100.07 |
| 54.14 | 97.08 |
| 49.12 | 91.59 |
| 40.71 | 94.85 |
| 55.15 | 94.65 |

*Program:*

```
/* Calculation corelation coefficient */
# include <stdio.h>
# include <math.h>
int main( )
{
    int n = 11, i, j ;
    float x[ 11 ] = { 34.22, 39.87, 41.85, 43.23, 40.06, 53.29, 53.29,
                    54.14, 49.12, 40.71, 55.15 } ;
    float y[ 11 ] = { 102.43, 100.93, 97.43, 97.81, 98.32, 98.32,
```

```
                    100.07, 97.08, 91.59, 94.85, 94.65 } ;
    float r ;
    float sx = 0.0, sxy = 0.0, sy = 0.0, sxs = 0.0, sys = 0.0 ;
    float r1, r2 ;
    for ( i = 0 ; i <= 10 ; i++ )
    {
        sx = sx + x[ i ] ; /* Summation of X */
        sxy = sxy + x[ i ] * y[ i ] ; /* Summation of XY */
        sy = sy + y[ i ] ; /* Summation of Y */
        sxs = sxs + x[ i ] * x[ i ] ; /* Summation of square of X */
        sys = sys + y[ i ] * y[ i ] ; /* Summation of square of Y */
    }
    printf ( "\n\n%c X   = %.2f\n", 228, sx ) ;
    printf ( "%c Y   = %.2f\n" , 228, sy ) ;
    printf ( "%c XY  = %.2f\n" , 228, sxy ) ;
    printf ( "%c X*X = %.2f\n" , 228, sxs ) ;
    printf ( "%c Y*Y = %.2f\n" , 228, sys ) ;
    r1 = ( sxy - sx * sy ) ;
    r2 = ( sqrt ( ( n * sxs - sx * sx ) * ( n * sys - sy * sy ) ) ) ;
    r = r1 / r2 ;
    printf ( "\n\n( Numerator ) r1  = %f\n", r1 ) ;
    printf ( "( Denominator) r2 = %f\n", r2 ) ;
    printf ( "Corelation coefficient r1/r2 = %f\n", r ) ;
    return 0 ;
}
```

(i) The **X** and **Y** coordinates of 10 different points are entered through the keyboard. Write a program to find the distance of last point from the first point (sum of distances between consecutive points).

*Program:*

```
/* Distance between two points */
# include <stdio.h>
# include <math.h>
int main( )
{
    int i, x[ 10 ], y[ 10 ] ;
    float sum = 0 ;
    printf ( "\nEnter the coordinates for the points: " ) ;
    for ( i = 0 ; i <= 9 ; i++ )
```

```
    {
        printf ( "\nX[ %d ] = ", i + 1 ) ;
        scanf ( "%d", &x[ i ] ) ;
        printf ( "Y[ %d ] = ", i + 1 ) ;
        scanf ( "%d", &y[ i ] ) ;
    }
    for ( i = 0 ; i <= 8 ; i++ )
        sum = sum + sqrt ( pow ( ( x[ i + 1 ] - x[ i ] ), 2 ) + pow ( (
                y[ i + 1 ] - y[ i ] ), 2 ) ) ;
    printf ( "\nDistance of the last point  from the first point  =
                %.2f\n", sum ) ;
    return 0 ;
}
```

(j) A dequeue is an ordered set of elements in which elements may be inserted or retrieved from either end. Using an array simulate a dequeue of characters and the operations retrieve left, retrieve right, insert left, insert right. Exceptional conditions such as dequeue full or empty should be reported. Use two pointers **left** and **right** for this simulation.

*Program:*

```
/* Implementation of a deque using an array */
# include <stdio.h>
void add_front ( int ) ;
void add_rear ( int ) ;
int  retrieve_front( ) ;
int  retrieve_rear( ) ;
void display( ) ;
int  *front, *rear ;
int  a[ 26 ] ;
int main( )
{
    int  item ;
    front = NULL ;
    rear = NULL ;
    printf ( "\nAdding elements at front of a deque: " ) ;
    add_front ( 10 ) ;
    add_front ( 40 ) ;
    add_front ( 30 ) ;
```

```
    display( ) ;
    printf ( "\n\nAdding an element at rear of a deque: " ) ;
    add_rear ( 50 ) ;
    display( ) ;
    printf ( "\n\nRetreiving an element from front of a deque: " ) ;
    item = retrieve_front( ) ;
    if ( item == -1 )
        printf ( "\nDeQueue Empty " ) ;
    else
        printf ( "\n\nFront Item = %d ", item ) ;
    display( ) ;
    printf ( "\n\nRetreiving an element from rear of a deque: " ) ;
    item = retrieve_rear( ) ;
    if ( item == -1 )
        printf ( "\nDeQueue Empty " ) ;
    else
        printf ( "\n\nRear Item = %d ", item ) ;
    display( ) ;
    return 0 ;
}
/* Function to retrieve item from rear */
int retrieve_rear( )
{
    int item, i, j ;
    if ( rear == NULL )
    {
        printf ( "\n DeQueue Empty " ) ;
        return -1 ;
    }
    else
    {
        item = *rear ;
        i = rear - front ;
        if ( i == 0 )
        {
            front = NULL ;
            rear = NULL ;
        }
        else
        {
            *rear = 0 ;
```

```
            rear-- ;
        }
    }
    return item ;
}
/* Function to retrieve item from front */
int  retrieve_front( )
{
    int  item, i, j ;
    if ( front == NULL )
    {
        printf ( "\n DeQueue Empty " ) ;
        return -1 ;
    }
    else
    {
        item = *front ;
        i = rear - front ;
        if ( i == 0 )
        {
            front = NULL ;
            rear = NULL ;
        }
        else
        {
            for ( j = 0 ; j <= i - 1 ; j ++ )
                front [ j ] = front [ j + 1 ] ;
            *rear = 0 ;
            rear-- ;
        }
    }
    return item ;
}
/* Function to add item to rear */
void add_rear ( int item )
{
    int  i, j ;
    if ( front == NULL )
    {
        front = a ;
        *front = item ;
```

```
            rear = a ;
        }
        else
        {
            i = rear - front ;
            if ( i != 25 )
            {
                rear++ ;
                *rear = item ;
            }
            else
                printf ( "\nDeQueue full " ) ;
        }
}
/* Function to add item at front */
void add_front ( int  item )
{
    int  i, j ;
    if ( front == NULL )
    {
        front = a ;
        *( front ) = item ;
        rear = a ;
    }
    else
    {
        front = a ;
        j = rear - front ;
        if ( j != 25 )
        {
            for ( i = j + 1 ; i >= 0 ; i-- )
                front [ i ] = front [ i - 1 ] ;
            *( front + 0 ) = item ;
            rear++ ;
        }
        else
            printf ( "\n DeQueue Full " ) ;
    }
}

/* Function to display the deque */
```

```
void display( )
{
    int i ;
    int *p = front ;
    if ( p == NULL )
    {
        printf ( "\n\nDeQueue Empty " ) ;
    }
    else
    {
        printf ( "\n" ) ;
        for ( i = 0 ; i <= ( rear - front ) ; i++ )
            printf ( "\n a[ %d ] = %d ", i, *p++ ) ;
    }
}
```

# CHAPTER

# FOURTEEN

# Multidimensional Arrays

**[A]** What will be the output of the following programs?

(a)
```
# include <stdio.h>
int main( )
{
    int n[ 3 ][ 3 ] = {
                        { 2, 4, 3 }, { 6, 8, 5 }, { 3, 5, 1 }
                    } ;
    printf ( "%d %d %d\n", *n, n[ 3 ][ 3 ], n[ 2 ][ 2 ] ) ;
    return 0 ;
}
```

*Output:*

<base address><garbage value> 1

(b)
```
# include <stdio.h>
int main( )
{
    int n[ 3 ][ 3 ] = {
                        { 2, 4, 3 }, { 6, 8, 5 }, { 3, 5, 1 }
                    } ;
    int i, *ptr ;
    ptr = &n[ 0 ][ 0 ] ;
```

```
    for ( i = 0 ; i <= 8 ; i++ )
        printf ( "%d\n", *( ptr + i ) ) ;
    return 0 ;
}
```

*Output:*

```
2
4
3
6
8
5
3
5
1
```

(c)
```
# include <stdio.h>
int main( )
{
    int n[ 3 ][ 3 ] = {
                        2, 4, 3, 6, 8, 5,3, 5, 1
                    } ;
    int i, j ;
    for ( i = 0 ; i <= 2 ; i++ )
        for ( j = 0 ; j <= 2 ; j++ )
            printf ( "%d %d\n", n[ i ][ j ], *( *( n + i ) + j ) ) ;
    return 0 ;
}
```

*Output:*

```
2 2
4 4
3 3
6 6
.....
....
1 1
```

**[B]** Point out the errors, if any, in the following programs:

(a)
```
# include <stdio.h>
int main( )
```

```
{
    int twod[ ][ ] = { 2, 4, 6, 8 } ;
    printf ( "%d\n", twod ) ;
    return 0 ;
}
```

Error. While declaring a two-dimensional array mentioning the column dimension is necessary.

(b)
```
# include <stdio.h>
int main( )
{
    int three[ 3 ][ ] = { { 2, 4, 3 }, { 6, 8, 2 }, { 2, 3, 1 } } ;
    printf ( "%d\n", three[ 1 ][ 1 ] ) ;
    return 0 ;
}
```

Error. While declaring a two-dimensional array mentioning the column dimension is necessary.

**[C]** Attempt the following questions:

(a) How will you initialize a three-dimensional array **threed[3][2][3]**? How will you refer the first and last element in this array?

*Answer:*

```
int arr[ 3 ][ 2 ][ 3 ] = {
                            {
                                { 1, 2, 3 },
                                { 4, 5, 6 }
                            },
                            {
                                { 1, 2, 3 },
                                { 4, 5, 6 }
                            },
                            {
                                { 1, 2, 3 },
                                { 4, 5, 6 }
                            }
                         } ;
```

The first element of the array is **arr[ 0 ][ 0 ][ 0 ]** or *****arr**. The last element of the array is **arr[ 2 ][ 1 ][ 2 ]** or ***(*(*(arr + 2) + 1 ) + 2)**.

(b) Match the following with reference to the following program segment:

```
int i, j, = 25 ;
int *pi, *pj = & j ;
*pj = j + 5 ;
j = *pj + 5 ;
pj = pj ;
*pi = i + j ;
```

Each integer quantity occupies 2 bytes of memory. The value assigned to **i** begins at (hexadecimal) address F9C and the value assigned to j begins at address F9E. Match the value represented by expressions in the left column with values in the right column.

| | | | |
|---|---|---|---|
| 1. | &i | a. | 30 |
| 2. | &j | b. | F9E |
| 3. | pj | c. | 35 |
| 4. | *pj | d. | FA2 |
| 5. | i | e. | F9C |
| 6. | pi | f. | 67 |
| 7. | *pi | g. | unspecified |
| 8. | ( pi + 2 ) | h. | 65 |
| 9. | (*pi + 2) | i. | F9E |
| 10. | * ( pi + 2 ) | j. | F9E |
| | | k. | FAO |
| | | l. | F9D |

*Answer*

| | | | |
|---|---|---|---|
| 1. | &i | e. | F9C |
| 2. | &j | b. | F9E |

| | | | |
|---|---|---|---|
| 3. | pj | i. | F9E |
| 4. | *pj | h. | 65 |
| 5. | i | c. | 35 |
| 6. | pi | j. | F9E |
| 7. | *pi | h. | 65 |
| 8. | (pi + 2 ) | d. | FA2 |
| 9. | (*pi + 2) | f. | 67 |
| 10. | * ( pi + 2 ) | g. | unspecified |

(c) Match the following with reference to the following program segment:

```
int  x[ 3 ][ 5 ] ={
                    { 1, 2, 3, 4, 5 },
                    { 6, 7, 8, 9, 10 },
                    { 11, 12, 13, 14, 15 }
                }, *n = &x ;
```

| | | | |
|---|---|---|---|
| 1. | *( *( x + 2 ) + 1) | a. | 9 |
| 2. | *( *x + 2 ) + 5 | b. | 13 |
| 3. | *( *( x + 1) ) | c. | 4 |
| 4. | *( *( x ) + 2 ) + 1 | d. | 3 |
| 5. | * ( *( x + 1 ) + 3 ) | e. | 2 |
| 6. | *n | f. | 12 |
| 7. | *( n +2 ) | g. | 14 |
| 8. | (*(n + 3 ) + 1 | h. | 7 |
| 9. | *(n + 5)+1 | i. | 1 |
| 10. | ++*n | j. | 8 |
| | | k. | 5 |
| | | l. | 10 |
| | | m. | 6 |

*Answer:*

| | | | |
|---|---|---|---|
| 1. | *(*( x + 2 ) + 1) | f. | 12 |
| 2. | *(*x + 2 ) + 5 | j. | 8 |
| 3. | *(*( x + 1) ) | m. | 6 |
| 4. | *(*(x) + 2 ) + 1 | c. | 4 |
| 5. | * ( *( x + 1 ) + 3 ) | a. | 9 |
| 6. | *n | i. | 1 |
| 7. | *( n +2 ) | d. | 3 |
| 8. | (*(n + 3 ) + 1 | k. | 5 |
| 9. | *(n + 5)+1 | h. | 7 |
| 10. | ++*n | e. | 2 |

(d) Match the following with reference to the following program segment:

```
unsigned int  arr[ 3 ][ 3 ] = {
                                2, 4, 6,
                                9, 1, 10,
                                16, 64, 5
                              };
```

| | | | |
|---|---|---|---|
| 1. | **arr | a. | 64 |
| 2. | **arr < *( *arr + 2 ) | b. | 18 |
| 3. | *( arr + 2 ) / ( *( *arr + 1 ) > **arr ) | c. | 6 |
| 4. | *( arr[ 1 ] + 1 ) \| arr[ 1 ][ 2 ] | d. | 3 |
| 5. | *( arr[ 0 ] ) \| *( arr[ 2 ] ) | e. | 0 |
| 6. | arr[ 1 ][ 1 ] < arr[ 0 ][ 1 ] | f. | 16 |
| 7. | arr[ 2 ][ [ 1 ] & arr[ 2 ][ 0 ] | g. | 1 |
| 8. | arr[ 2 ][ 2 ] \| arr[ 0 ][ 1 ] | h. | 11 |
| 9. | arr[ 0 ][ 1 ] ^ arr[ 0 ][ 2 ] | i. | 20 |
| 10. | ++**arr + --arr[ 1 ][ 1 ] | j. | 2 |

k. 5

l. 4

*Answer:*

1. **arr — j. 2
2. **arr < *(*arr + 2 ) — g. 1
3. *(arr + 2) / ( *(*arr + 1) > **arr ) — c. 6
4. *( arr[ 1 ] + 1) | arr[ 1 ][ 2 ] — h. 11
5. *(arr[ 0 ]) | *(arr[ 2 ]) — b. 18
6. arr[ 1 ][ 1 ] < arr[ 0 ][ 1 ] — g. 1
7. arr[ 2 ][ [ 1 ] & arr[ 2 ][ 0 ] — e. 0
8. arr[ 2 ][ 2 ] | arr[ 0 ][ 1 ] — k. 5
9. arr[ 0 ][ 1 ] ^ arr[ 0 ][ 2 ] — j. 2
10. ++**arr + --arr[ 1 ][ 1 ] — d. 3

(e) Write a program to find if a square matrix is symmetric.

*Program:*

```
/* To check if a square matrix is symmetric */
# include <stdio.h>
int main( )
{
    int arr[ 3 ][ 3 ], i, j, count = 0 ;

    printf ( "\nEnter the elements of the Matrix:\n" ) ;
    for ( i = 0 ; i <= 2 ; i++ )
    {
        for ( j = 0 ; j <= 2 ; j++ )
            scanf ( "%d", &arr[ i ][ j ] ) ;
    }
    printf ( "\nThe matrix formed is....\n" ) ;
    for ( i = 0 ; i <= 2 ; i++ )
    {
        for ( j = 0 ; j <= 2 ; j++ )
```

```
            printf ( "%d  ", arr[ i ][ j ] ) ;
        printf ( "\n" ) ;
    }
    /* Check for symmetry */
    for ( i = 0 ; i <= 2 ; i++ )
    {
        for ( j = i ; j <= 2 ; j++ )
        {
            if ( arr[ i ][ j ] == arr[ j ][ i ] )
                count++ ;
        }
    }
    if ( count == 6 )
        printf ( "\n\nThe matrix is symmetric\n" ) ;
    else
        printf ( "\n\nThe matrix is not symmetric\n" ) ;

    return 0 ;
}
```

(f) Write a program to add two 6 x 6 matrices.

*Program:*

```
/* Program to add two 6 x 6 matrices */
# include <stdio.h>
int main( )
{
    int  mat1[ 6 ][ 6 ], mat2[ 6 ][ 6 ], mat3[ 6 ][ 6 ], i, j ;
    printf ( "\nEnter values for first 6 x 6 matrix:\n" ) ;
    for ( i = 0 ; i <= 5 ; i++ )
    {
        for ( j = 0 ; j <= 5 ; j++ )
            scanf ( "%d", &mat1[ i ][ j ] ) ;  /* Enter 1st Matrix */
    }
    printf ( "\nEnter values for second 6 x 6 matrix:\n" ) ;
    for ( i = 0 ; i <= 5 ; i++ )
    {
        for ( j = 0 ; j <= 5 ; j++ )
            scanf ( "%d", &mat2[ i ][ j ] ) ;  /* Enter 2nd Matrix */
    }
```

```
    /* print both matrices as entered */
    printf ( "\nMatrices entered by you are: \nMatrix 1:\n" ) ;
    for ( i = 0 ; i <= 5 ; i++ )
    {
        for ( j = 0 ; j <= 5 ; j++ )
            printf ( "%d\t", mat1[ i ][ j ] ) ; /* print each row */
        printf ( "\n" ) ; /* new row on new line */
    }
    printf ( "\nMatrix 2:\n" ) ;
    for ( i = 0 ; i <= 5 ; i++ )
    {
        for ( j = 0 ; j <= 5 ; j++ )
            printf ( "%d\t", mat2[ i ][ j ] ) ; /* print each row */
        printf ( "\n" ) ; /* new row on new line */
    }
    /* Calculate the sum of two matrices */
    for ( i = 0 ; i <= 5 ; i++ )
    {
        for ( j = 0 ; j <= 5 ; j++ )
            mat3[ i ][ j ] = mat1[ i ][ j ] + mat2[ i ][ j ] ;
    }
    /* print the matrix with the sum */
    printf ( "\nThe new matrix after addition of the above two
            matrices is:\n" ) ;
    for ( i = 0 ; i <= 5 ; i++ )
    {
        for ( j = 0 ; j <= 5 ; j++ )
            printf ( "%d\t", mat3[ i ][ j ] ) ;
        printf ( "\n" ) ;
    }
    return 0 ;
}
```

(g) Write a program to multiply any two 3 x 3 matrices.

*Program:*

```
/* Program to multiply two 3 x 3 matrices */
# include <stdio.h>
int main( )
{
```

```
int  mat1[ 3 ][ 3 ], mat2[ 3 ][ 3 ], mat3[ 3 ][ 3 ], i, j, k, sum ;
/* get values for first matrix */
printf ( "\nEnter values for first 3 x 3 matrix:\n" ) ;
for ( i = 0 ; i <= 2 ; i++ )
{
    for ( j = 0 ; j <= 2 ; j++ )
        scanf ( "%d", &mat1[ i ][ j ] ) ;
}
/* get values for second matrix */
printf ( "\nEnter values for second 3 x 3 matrix:\n" ) ;
for ( i = 0 ; i <= 2 ; i++ )
{
    for ( j = 0 ; j <= 2 ; j++ )
        scanf ( "%d", &mat2[ i ][ j ] ) ;
}
/* print the first matrix as entered */
printf ( "\nThe first 3 x 3 matrix entered by you is:\n" ) ;
for ( i = 0 ; i <= 2 ; i++ )
{
    for ( j = 0 ; j <= 2 ; j++ )
        printf ( "%d\t", mat1[ i ][ j ] ) ;
    printf ( "\n" ) ;
}
/* print the second matrix as entered */
printf ( "\nThe second 3 x 3 matrix entered by you is:\n" ) ;
for ( i = 0 ; i <= 2 ; i++ )
{
    for ( j = 0 ; j <= 2 ; j++ )
        printf ( "%d\t", mat2[ i ][ j ] ) ;
    printf ( "\n" ) ;
}
/* calculate the product of the two matrices */
for ( i = 0 ; i <= 2 ; i++ )
{
    for ( j = 0 ; j <= 2 ; j++ )
    {
        sum = 0 ;
        for ( k = 0 ; k <= 2 ; k++ )
            sum = sum + mat1[ i ][ k ] * mat2[ k ][ j ] ;
        mat3[ i ][ j ] = sum ;
    }
```

```
    }
    /* print the new matrix containing the product */
    printf ( "\nThe product of the above two matrices is:\n" ) ;
    for ( i = 0 ; i <= 2 ; i++ )
    {
        for ( j = 0 ; j <= 2 ; j++ )
            printf ( "%d\t", mat3[ i ][ j ] ) ;
        printf ( "\n" ) ;
    }
    return 0 ;
}
```

(h) Given an array **p[ 5 ]**, write a function to shift it circularly left by two positions. Thus, if the original array is { 15, 30, 28, 19, 61 } then after shifting it will be { 28, 19, 61, 15, 30 } Call this function for a 4 x 5 matrix and get its rows left shifted.

*Program:*

```
/* Circular rotation of array elements and its use in matrix */
# include <stdio.h>
void swap ( int * ) ;
int main( )
{
    int p[ 4 ][ 5 ] ;
    int i, j ;
    /* Enter data for a matrix */
    for ( i = 0 ; i <= 3 ; i++ )
    {
        printf ( "\nEnter the %d row elements:\n", i ) ;
        for ( j = 0 ; j <= 4 ; j++ )
        {
            scanf ( "%d", &p[ i ][ j ] ) ;
        }
    }
    /* Print matrix as entered */
    printf ( "\nMatrix elements as entered:" ) ;
    for ( i = 0 ; i <= 3 ; i++ )
    {
        printf ( "\nThe %d row elements:  ", i ) ;
        for ( j = 0 ; j <= 4 ; j++ )
```

```
            printf ( "\t%d", p[ i ][ j ] ) ;
    }
    printf ( "\n" ) ;
    /* Function call to left shift rows */
    swap ( p ) ; /* Base address of array passed to function */

    /* Print new matrix after left shifting */
    printf ( "\nMatrix after left shifting the row elements:" ) ;
    for ( i = 0 ; i <= 3 ; i++ )
    {
        printf ( "\nThe %d row elements:  ", i ) ;
        for ( j = 0 ; j <= 4 ; j++ )
            printf ( "\t%d", p[ i ][ j ] ) ;
    }
    return 0 ;
}
/* Function for left shifting of the rows */
void swap ( int  *p )
{
    int  k, i, tt, t, j ;
    for ( k = 0 ; k <= 3 ; k++ )  /* 4 rows to be shifted */
    {
        for ( i = 0 ; i <= 1 ; i++ )  /* shifting done twice */
        {
            t = *( p + k * 5 + 0 )  ;
            for ( j = 0 ; j <= 3 ; j++ )
            {
                tt = *( p + k * 5 + j ) ;
                *( p + k * 5 + j ) = *( p + k * 5 + j + 1 ) ;
                *( p + k * 5 + j + 1 )  = tt ;
            }
            *( p + k * 5 + j ) = t ;
        }
    }
}
```

# CHAPTER FIFTEEN

# Strings

**[A]** What will be the output of the following programs?

(a)
```
# include <stdio.h>
int main( )
{
    char c[ 2 ] = "A" ;
    printf ( "%c\n", c[ 0 ] ) ;
    printf ( "%s\n", c ) ;
    return 0 ;
}
```

*Output:*

```
A
A
```

(b)
```
# include <stdio.h>
int main( )
{
    char s[ ] = "Get organised! learn C!!" ;
    printf ( "%s\n", &s[ 2 ] ) ;
    printf ( "%s\n", s ) ;
    printf ( "%s\n", &s ) ;
    printf ( "%c\n", s[ 2 ] ) ;
    return 0 ;
}
```

*Output:*

```
t orgainsed ! learn c !!
Get organised ! learn c !!
```

```
Get orgainsed ! learn c !!
t
```

(c)
```
# include <stdio.h>
int main( )
{
    char  s[  ] = "Borrowers of books spoil the symmetry of shelves" ;
    int  i = 0 ;
    while ( s[ i ] != 0 )
    {
        printf ( "%c %c\n", s[ i ], *( s + i ) ) ;
        printf ( "%c %c\n", i[ s ], *( i + s ) ) ;
        i++ ;
    }
    return 0 ;
}
```

*Output:*

```
B  B
B  B
o  o
o  o
r  r
r  r
......
......
s  s
s  s
```

(d)
```
# include <stdio.h>
int main( )
{
    char str1[ ] = { 'H', 'e', 'l', 'l', 'o', 0 } ;
    char str2[ ] = "Hello" ;
    printf ( "%s\n", str1 ) ;
    printf ( "%s\n", str2 ) ;
    return 0 ;
}
```

*Output:*

Hello
Hello

(e)
```
# include <stdio.h>
int main( )
{
    printf ( 5 + "Good Morning " ) ;
    printf ( "%c\n", "abcdefgh"[ 4 ] ) ;
    return 0 ;
}
```

*Output:*

Morning e

(f)
```
# include <stdio.h>
int main( )
{
    printf ( "%d %d %d\n", sizeof ( '3' ), sizeof ( "3" ), sizeof ( 3 ) ) ;
    return 0 ;
}
```

*Output:*

4 2 4

**[B]** Fill in the blanks:

(a) "A" is a <u>string</u> whereas 'A' is a <u>character</u>.

(b) A string is terminated by a <u>null</u> character, which is written as <u>\0</u>.

(c) The array **char name[10]** can consist of a maximum of <u>9</u> characters.

(d) The array elements are always stored in <u>consecutive</u> memory locations.

**[C]** Attempt the following questions:

(a) If the string "Alice in wonder land" is fed to the following **scanf( )** statement, what will be the contents of arrays **str1**, **str2**, **str3** and **str4**?

```
char str1[ 20 ], str2[ 20 ], str3[ 20 ], str4[ 20 ] ;
scanf ( "%s%s%s%s", str1, str2, str3, str4 ) ;
```

*Answer:*

str1 – Alice
str2 – in
str3 – wonder
str4 – land

(b) To uniquely identify a book a 10-digit ISBN number is used. The rightmost digit in ISBN is a checksum digit. This digit is determined from the other 9 digits using the condition that $d_1 + 2d_2 + 3d_3 + ... + 10d_{10}$ must be a multiple of 11 (where $d_i$ denotes the $i^{th}$ digit from the right). The checksum digit $d_1$ can be any value from 0 to 10: the ISBN convention is to use the value X to denote 10. Write a program that receives a 10-digit integer, computes the checksum, and reports whether the ISBN number is correct or not.

*Program:*

```
/* Check correctness of ISBN number */
#include <stdio.h>
#include <string.h>
int main( )
{
    char str[ 11 ] ;
    int i, j, sum ;
    printf ( "Enter 10 digit ISBN number: " ) ;
    scanf ( "%s", str ) ;
    j = 2 ;
    sum = 0 ;
    for ( i = 8 ; i >= 0 ; i-- )
    {
        sum = sum + ( str [ i ] - '0' ) * j ;
        j++ ;
    }
    for ( i = 0 ; i <= 9 ; i++ )
    {
        if ( ( sum + i ) % 11 == 0 )
            break ;
```

```
    }
    if ( i == str[ 9 ] - '0' )
        printf ( "ISBN Number is verified & found to be correct\n" ) ;
    else
        printf ( "Checksum error in ISBN Number\n" ) ;
    return 0 ;
}
```

(c) A Credit Card number is usually a 16-digit number. A valid Credit Card number would satisfy a rule explained below with the help of a dummy Credit Card number—4567 1234 5678 9129. Start with the rightmost - 1 digit and multiply every other digit by 2.

4567 1 2 3 4 5 6 7 8 9 1 2 9

8 12 2 6 10 14 18 4

Then subtract 9 from numbers that are larger than 10. Thus, we get:

8 3 2 6 1 5 9 4

Add them all up to get 38.

Add all the other digits to get 42.

Sum of 38 and 42 is 80. Since 80 is divisible by 10, the Credit Card number is valid.

Write a program that receives a Credit Card number and checks using the above rule whether the Credit Card number is valid.

*Program:*

```
/* Verify correctness of Credit Card Number */
#include <stdio.h>
#include <string.h>
int main( )
{
    int len, i, sum, digit, multiple ;
    char str[ 20 ] ;
    printf ( "Enter the Credit Card number: " ) ;
    scanf ( "%s", str ) ;
```

```
    len = strlen ( str ) ;
    sum = 0 ;
    for ( i = 15 ; i >= 0 ; i-- )
    {
        digit = str[ i ] - '0';
        if ( i % 2 == 0 )
        {
            multiple = digit * 2 ;
            digit = multiple < 10 ? multiple : multiple - 9 ;
        }
        sum += digit ;
    }
    printf ( "%d\n", sum ) ;

    if ( sum % 10 == 0 )
        printf ( "Valid credit card number\n" ) ;
    else
        printf ( "Invalid credit card number\n" ) ;
    return 0 ;
}
```

# CHAPTER SIXTEEN

# Handling Multiple Strings

**[A]** Answer the following questions:

(a) How many bytes in memory would be occupied by the following array of pointers to strings? How many bytes would be required to store the same strings in a two-dimensional character array?

```
char *mess[ ] =  {
                     "Hammer and tongs",
                     "Tooth and nail",
                     "Spit and polish",
                     "You and C"
                 } ;
```

*Answer:*

58 bytes for storing strings using array of pointers
68 bytes for storing strings using two-dimensional array

(b) Write a program to delete all vowels from a sentence. Assume that the sentence is not more than 80 characters long.

*Program:*

```
/* Delete all vowels from a sentence */
# include <stdio.h>
int main( )
{
    char str[ 80 ], str1[ 80 ] ;
    char *s, *p ;
```

```
    printf ( "\nEnter a sentence of max 80 characters:\n" ) ;
    gets ( str ) ;
    s = str ;
    p = str1 ;
    while ( *s )
    {
        if ( *s == 'a' || *s == 'e' || *s == 'i' || *s == 'o' || *s == 'u' )
            s++ ;
        else
        if ( *s == 'A' || *s == 'E' || *s == 'I' || *s == 'O' || *s == 'U' )
            s++ ;
        else
            *p++ = *s++ ;
    }
    *p = '\0' ;
    printf ( "\n\nSentence after removing all vowels is:\n" ) ;
    puts ( str1 ) ;
    return 0 ;
}
```

(c) Write a program that will read a line and delete from it all occurrences of the word ‘the’.

*Program:*

```
/* Delete all occurrences of "the" from a sentence */
# include <stdio.h>
int main( )
{
    char  str[ 80 ], str2[ 80 ] ;
    char *s, *q, *p ;
    int  i ;
    printf ( "\nEnter a sentence not more than 80 chars long:\n" ) ;
    gets ( str ) ;
    s = str ;  /* Base address of the string */
    p = str2 ;  /* Base address of new string */
    while ( *s )
    {
        q = s ;
        if ( *s == 't' || *s == 'T' )
        {
```

```
                s++ ;
                if ( *s == 'h' )
                {
                    s++ ;
                    if ( *s == 'e' )
                    ;
                    else
                    {
                        for ( i = 0; i <= 2 ; i++ )
                            *p++ = *q++ ;
                    }
                }
                else
                {
                    *p++ = *q++ ;
                    s-- ;
                }
            }
            else
                *p++ = *s ;
            s++ ;
        }
        *p = '\0' ;
        printf ( "\nSentence after deleting all occurences of 'the' is:\n" ) ;
        puts ( str2 ) ;
        return 0 ;
    }
```

(d) Write a program that stores a set of names of individuals and abbreviates the first, middle and other names except the last name by their first letter.

*Program:*

```
/* Convert a full name into initials & last name */
# include <stdio.h>
# include <string.h>
int main( )
{
    char  str1[ 30 ], str2[ 30 ], target[ 30 ] ;
    char lastname[ 20 ] ;
```

```
    char *p, *token ;
    int count, i, j ;
    printf ( "\nEnter name, middle name and surname:\n" ) ;
    gets ( str1 ) ;
    strcpy ( str2, str1 ) ;
    count = 0 ;
    token = strtok ( str1, " " ) ;
    while ( token != NULL )
    {
        count++ ;
        token = strtok ( NULL, " " ) ;
    }

    j = 0 ;
    i = 0 ;
    p = strtok ( str2, " " ) ;
    while ( p != NULL )
    {
        if ( i == count - 1 )
        {
            strcpy ( lastname, p ) ;
            target[ j ] = '\0' ;
        }
        else
        {
            target[ j ] = *p ;
            j++ ;
            target[ j ] = '.' ;
            j++ ;
        }
        i++ ;
        p = strtok ( NULL, " " ) ;
    }
    strcat ( target, lastname ) ;
    printf ( "%s\n", target ) ;
    return 0 ;
}
```

(e) Write a program to count the number of occurrences of any two vowels in succession in a line of text. For example, in the sentence

"Please read this application and give me gratuity"

such occurrences are ea, ea, ui.

*Program:*

```
/* Check for 2 vowels in succession */
# include <stdio.h>
int main( )
{
    char str[ 80 ] ;
    int count = 0 ;
    char *s = str ;

    printf ( "\nEnter the string:\n" ) ;
    gets ( str ) ;
    while ( *s )
    {
        if ( *s == 'a' || *s == 'e' || *s == 'i' || *s == 'o' || *s == 'u' )
        {
            s++ ;
            if ( *s == 'a' || *s == 'e' || *s == 'i' || *s == 'o' ||
                    *s == 'u' )
                count ++ ;
        }
        s++ ;
    }
    printf ( "No. of occurrences: %d\n" , count ) ;
    return 0 ;
}
```

(f) Write a program that receives an integer (less than or equal to nine digits in length) and prints out the number in words. For example, if the number input is 12342, then the output should be Twelve Thousand Three Hundred Forty Two.

*Program:*

```
/* Convert number to words */
#include<stdio.h>
void convert ( long, char [ ] ) ;
char *one[ ] = {
                    " ", " One"," Two"," Three"," Four"," Five",
```

```
                    " Six"," Seven", "Eight"," Nine"," Ten",
                    " Eleven"," Twelve"," Thirteen"," Fourteen",
                    "Fifteen"," Sixteen"," Seventeen"," Eighteen",
                    " Nineteen"
                } ;
char *ten[ ] = {
                    " ", " ", " Twenty"," Thirty"," Forty"," Fifty",
                    " Sixty", "Seventy"," Eighty"," Ninety"
                } ;
int main( )
{
    long num ;
    printf ( "\nEnter any Number (max 9 digits): " ) ;
    scanf ( "%ld", &num ) ;
    if ( num <= 0 )
        printf ( "No negative numbers please...\n" ) ;
    else
    {
        convert ( ( num / 10000000 ), "Crore" ) ;
        convert ( ( ( num / 100000 ) % 100 ), "Lakh" ) ;
        convert ( ( ( num / 1000 ) % 100 ), "Thousand" ) ;
        convert ( ( ( num / 100 ) % 10 ), "Hundred" ) ;
        convert ( ( num % 100 )," " ) ;
    }
}
void convert ( long n, char *s )
{
    if ( n > 19 )
        printf ( "%s %s ", ten[ n / 10 ], one[ n % 10 ] ) ;
    else
        printf ( "%s ", one[ n ] ) ;
    if ( n )
        printf ( "%s ", s ) ;
}
```

# CHAPTER SEVENTEEN

# Structures

**[A]** Answer the following questions:

(a) Given the statement,

maruti.engine.bolts = 25 ;

which of the following is True?

(1) bolts is a structure variable
(2) engine is a structure variable
(3) maruti is a structure variable
(4) (2) and (3)

*Answer:*

(4)

(b)
```
struct time
{
   int hours ; int minutes ; int seconds ;
} t ;
struct time *pt ;
pt = &t ;
```

With reference to above declarations which of the following refers to **seconds** correctly:

(1) pt.seconds
(2) ( *pt ).seconds
(3) time.seconds
(4) pt -> seconds

*Answer:*

(1) 4. tt -> seconds

**[B]** Attempt the following questions:

(a) Create a structure called **student** that can contain data given below:

Roll number, Name, Department, Course, Year of joining

Assume that there are not more than 450 students in the college.

(1) Write a function to print names of all students who joined in a particular year.

(2) Write a function to print the data of a student whose roll number is received by the function.

*Program:*

```
/* create structure to hold student data */
# include <stdio.h>
struct stud
{
    int r_n ; /* Roll Number */
    char name[ 20 ] ; /* Name */
    char dep[ 15 ] ; /* Department */
    char course[ 10 ] ; /* Course */
    int y_o_j ; /* Year Of Joining */
} ;
struct stud s[ 450 ] ; /* array of structure */
void set_student_data( ) ;
void display( ) ;
void name_acc_year ( int ) ;
void data_acc_rollno ( int ) ;
int main( )
{
    int i, r ;
    int y ;
    printf ( "\nEnter the data for each Student:\n\n " ) ;
    /* Initialize the values for the students structure */
    set_student_data( ) ;
    /* Display all the elements of the student structure */
    display( ) ;
    /* Search data on year of Joining */
```

```
    printf ( "\nEnter the Year of Joining of the Student " ) ;
    scanf ( "%d", &y ) ;
    name_acc_year ( y ) ;
    /* Search data based on roll number */
    printf ( "\nEnter the Roll Number of the Student" ) ;
    scanf ( "%d", &r ) ;
    data_acc_rollno ( r ) ;  /* roll number passed to function */
    return 0 ;
}
void set_student_data( )  /* Enter student data */
{
    int  i ;
    for ( i = 0 ; i < 450 ; i++ )
    {
        fflush ( stdin ) ;  /* Flush the input buffer */
        printf ( "\nEnter the Roll NUmber of the student\n" ) ;
        scanf ( "%d", &s[ i ].r_n ) ;
        fflush ( stdin ) ;
        printf ( "Enter the name of the student\n" ) ;
        scanf ( "%s", s[ i ].name ) ;
        fflush ( stdin ) ;
        printf ( "Enter the name of the Department\n" ) ;
        scanf ( "%s", s[ i ].dep ) ;
        fflush ( stdin ) ;
        printf ( "Enter the name of the Course\n" ) ;
        scanf ( "%s", s[ i ].course ) ;
        fflush ( stdin ) ;
        printf ( "Enter the Year of Joining of the student\n" ) ;
        scanf ( "%d", &s[ i ].y_o_j ) ;
    }
}
/* function to display data */
void display( )
{
    int  i ;
    for ( i = 0 ; i < 450 ; i++ )
    {
        printf ( "\nRoll Number %d =  %d \n", i+1 , s[ i ].r_n ) ;
        printf ( "\nName of student %d = %s \n", i+1, s[ i ].name ) ;
        printf ( "\nName of the Department = %s \n", s[ i ].dep ) ;
        printf ( "\nName of the Course = %s \n", s[ i ].course ) ;
```

```
            printf ( "\nYear of Joining %d = %d \n\n", i+1 , s[ i ].y_o_j ) ;
        }
}
/* function to get name based on year of joining */
void name_acc_year ( int  y )
{
    int  i, j = 0 ;
    for ( i = 0 ; i < 450 ; i++ )
    {
        if ( y == s[ i ].y_o_j )
        {
            printf ( "%s joined in the year %d\n", s[ i ].name,
                    s[ i ].y_o_j ) ;
            j = 1 ;
        }
    }
    if ( j == 0 )
        printf ( "\nNo student joined in the year %d", y ) ;
}
/* function to get student data based on roll number */
void  data_acc_rollno ( int r )
{
    int i, j = 0 ;
    for ( i = 0 ; i < 450 ; i++ )
    {
        if ( s[ i ].r_n == r )
        {
            printf ( "\n\tRoll Number of student =  %d \n", s[ i ].r_n ) ;
            printf ( "\n\tName of student = %s \n", s[ i ].name ) ;
            printf ( "\n\tDepartment = %s \n", s[ i ].dep ) ;
            printf ( "\n\tName of the Course = %s \n", s[ i ].course ) ;
            printf ( "\n\tYear of Joining = %d \n\n", s[ i ].y_o_j ) ;
            j = 1 ;
        }
    }
    if ( j == 0 )
        printf ( "\nNo such Roll Number present." ) ;
}
```

(b) Create a structure that can contain data of customers in a bank. The data to be stored is Account number, Name and Balance in account. Assume maximum of 200 customers in the bank.

(1) Define a function to print the Account number and name of each customer with balance below Rs. 1000.

(2) If a customer requests for withdrawal or deposit, it should receive as input Account number, amount and code (1 for deposit, 0 for withdrawal).

Define a function that prints a message, "The balance is insufficient for the specified withdrawal", if on withdrawal the balance falls below Rs. 1000.

*Program:*

```
/* Create structure of 200 customer's banks data */
# include <stdio.h>
/* function to link the floating point formats */
void fun( )
{
    float f, *ff = &f ;
}
/* structure for customer */
struct customer
{
    int acc_no ;
    char name[ 20 ] ;
    float bal_i_acc ;
} ;
struct customer cust[ 200 ] ;
/* function prototypes */
void with_dep ( int ano, float amount ) ;
void deposit ( int ano, float amount ) ;
void withdrawal ( int ano, float amount ) ;
void low_bal( ) ;
void display( ) ;
void set_cust_data( ) ;
int main( )
{
    int i, ano, choice ;
    float amount ;
```

```
    /* initialise Customer record */
    set_cust_data( ) ;
    /* display record of all the customers */
    display( ) ;
    /* print name and account number of the customer
       whose balance is less then 1000 */
    low_bal( ) ;
    /* withdraw or deposit the amount in account */
    printf ( "\nEnter acco number and amount: " ) ;
    scanf ( "%d%f", &ano, &amount ) ;
    with_dep ( ano, amount ) ;
    /*display all the records of the customers*/
    display( ) ;
    return 0 ;
}
void with_dep ( int  ano, float  amount )
{
    int  choice ;
    printf ( "Enter 1 for Deposit\t \tEnter 0 for Withdrawal" ) ;
    scanf ( "%d", &choice ) ;
    switch ( choice )
    {
        case 1 :
            deposit ( ano, amount ) ;
            break ;
        case 0 :
            withdrawal ( ano, amount ) ;
            break ;
        default :
            printf ( "You entered wrong choice\n" ) ;
    }
}
void deposit ( int  ano, float  amount )
{
    int  i, j = 0 ;
    for ( i = 0 ; i < 200 ; i++ )
    {
        if ( cust[ i ].acc_no == ano )
        {
            cust[ i ].bal_i_acc += amount ;
```

```
            j = 1 ;
        }
    }
    if ( j == 0 )
        printf ( "\n\tWrong Account Number\n" ) ;
}
void withdrawal ( int ano, float amount )
{
    int i, j = 0 ;
    for ( i = 0 ; i < 200 ; i++ )
    {
        if ( cust[ i ].acc_no == ano )
        {
            j = 1 ;
            if ( cust[ i ].bal_i_acc < 1000 )
            {
                printf ( "\n\t\tThe Balance is insufficient for the
                        specified Withdrawal\n" ) ;
            }
            else
                if ( cust[ i ].bal_i_acc - 1000 >= amount )
                    cust[ i ].bal_i_acc -= amount ;
                else
                    printf ( "\nwithdrawal amount should be <= %f
                            Rs.\n", cust[ i ].bal_i_acc - 1000 ) ;
        }
    }
    if ( j == 0 )
        printf ( "\n\tWrong Account Number\n" ) ;
}
void low_bal( )
{
    int i, j = 0 ;
    printf ( "\n\nName and Account no. with balance < 100\n" ) ;
    for ( i = 0 ; i < 200 ; i++ )
    {
        if ( cust[ i ].bal_i_acc < 1000 )
        {
            j = 1 ;
            printf ( "\tCustomer Number = %d\n", i+1 ) ;
            printf ( "\t\tAccount Number of Customer = %d\n",
```

```
                    cust[ i ].acc_no ) ;
            printf ( "\t\tName of Customer = %s\n", cust[ i ].name ) ;
        }
    }
    if ( j == 0 )
        printf ( "\n\tAll customers have sufficient balance\n" ) ;
}
void display( )
{
    int i ;
    for ( i = 0 ; i < 200 ; i++ )
    {
        printf ( "\n\n\tCustomer Number = %d\n", i+1 ) ;
        printf ( "\tAccount Number of Customer = %d\n",
                cust[ i ].acc_no ) ;
        printf ( "\tName of Customer = %s\n", cust[ i ].name ) ;
        printf ( "\tBalance Amount of Customer = %.3f\n",
                cust[ i ].bal_i_acc ) ;
    }
}
void set_cust_data( )
{
    int i ;
    for ( i = 0 ; i < 200 ; i++  )
    {
        printf ( "\n\nEnter Account number of the Customer\n\t" ) ;
        scanf ( "%d", &cust[ i ].acc_no ) ;
        fflush ( stdin ) ;
        printf ( "\nEnter the name of the Customer\n\t" ) ;
        scanf ( "%s", cust[ i ].name ) ;
        fflush ( stdin ) ;
        printf ( "\nEnter balance amount in account\n\t" ) ;
        scanf ( "%f", &cust[ i ].bal_i_acc ) ;
    }
}
```

(c) An automobile company has serial number for engine parts starting from AA0 to FF9. The other characteristics of parts are Year of manufacture, material and quantity manufactured.

(1) Specify a structure to store information corresponding to a part.

(2) Write a program to retrieve information on parts with serial numbers between BB1 and CC6.

*Program:*

```
/* Create structure to store engine parts data */
# include <stdio.h>
struct automobile
{
    int s_no ;
    int year_o_manu ;
    char material[ 20 ] ;
    int quantity ;
} ;

struct automobile part[ 2 ] ;
void retrieve( ) ;
void display( ) ;
void set_auto_data( ) ;
int main( )
{
    int i ;
    /* set the values for the records*/
    set_auto_data( ) ;
    /* list all the records*/
    display( ) ;

    /* retrieve info on parts from BB1 to CC6*/
    retrieve( ) ;
    return 0 ;
}
void retrieve( )
{
    int i, j = 0 ;
    printf ( "\nList of parts between BB1 & CC6:" ) ;
    for ( i = 0 ; i < 2 ; i++ )
    {
        if ( ( part[ i ].s_no >= 0xbb1 ) && ( part[ i ].s_no <= 0xcc6 ) )
        {
            j = 1 ;
            printf ( "\n\n\tPart Number = %d", i ) ;
            printf ( "\nSerial Number = %x", part[ i ].s_no ) ;
```

```
            printf ( "\nYear of manufacturing = %d",
                        part[ i ].year_o_manu ) ;
            printf ( "\nMaterial used : %s", part[ i ].material ) ;
            printf ( "\nMfg Quantity = %d", part[ i ].quantity ) ;
        }
    }
    if ( j == 0 )
        printf ( "\nNo such record present" ) ;
}
void display( )
{
    int i ;
    for ( i = 0 ; i < 2 ; i++ )
    {
        printf ( "\n\n\tPart Number = %d", i ) ;
        printf ( "\nSerial Number = %x", part[ i ].s_no ) ;
        printf ( "\nYear of mfg = %d", part[ i ].year_o_manu ) ;
        printf ( "\nMaterial used : %s", part[ i ].material ) ;
        printf ( "\nManufacture Quantity = %d", part[ i ].quantity ) ;
    }
}
void set_auto_data( )
{
    int i ;
    for ( i = 0 ; i < 2 ; i++ )
    {
        while ( 1 )
        {
            printf ( "\nEnter the serial Number of the part" ) ;
            printf ( "\nNumber must be between AA0 and FF9 " ) ;
            scanf ( "%x", &part[ i ].s_no ) ;
            if ( part[ i ].s_no >= 0xAA0 && part[ i ].s_no <= 0xff9 )
                break ;
        }
        printf ( "\nEnter the Year of manufacturing of the part" ) ;
        scanf ( "%d", &part[ i ].year_o_manu ) ;
        printf ( "\nEnter the material of the part" ) ;
        scanf ( "%s", &part[ i ].material ) ;
        fflush ( stdin ) ;
        printf ( "\nEnter the quantity of the part" ) ;
        scanf ( "%d", &part[ i ].quantity ) ;
```

```
    }
}
```

(d) A record contains name of cricketer, his age, number of test matches that he has played and the average runs that he has scored. Create an array of structures to hold records of 20 such cricketers and then write a program to read these records and arrange them in ascending order by average runs. Use the **qsort( )** standard library function.

*Program:*

```
/* Create array of structures, sort and display */
# include <malloc.h>
# include <stdio.h>
# include <stdlib.h>
void fun( ) ;
int sort_fun ( const void *, const void * ) ;
void sortbyavg( ) ;
void display( ) ;
void setdata( ) ;
/* Function to link the floating point formats */
void fun( )
{
    float f, *ff = &f ;
}
struct cric_player
{
    char name[ 20 ] ;
    int age ;
    int notest ;
    float avgrun ;
} ;
struct cric_player cp[ 3 ] ;
int main( )
{
    /* set the values of the structure elements */
    setdata( ) ;
    /* display all the entries present in the structure */
    printf ( "\nData as entered : \n" ) ;
    display( ) ;
    /* sort the array of structures */
```

```
    sortbyavg( ) ;
    printf ( "\nData sorted on Average Runs :\n" ) ;
    display( ) ;
    return 0 ;
}
/* Function used for sorting the array of structures */
void sortbyavg( )
{
    int i, j ;
    struct cric_player t ;
    qsort ( ( struct cric_player * ) cp, 3, sizeof ( cp[ 0 ] ), sort_fun ) ;
}
int sort_fun ( const void *f, const void *ff )
{
    return ( ( ( struct cric_player *) f ) -> avgrun -
                ( ( struct cric_player * ) ff ) -> avgrun ) ;
}
/* Function to display all the entries present in the structure */
void display( )
{
    int i ;
    for ( i = 0 ; i < 3 ; i++ )
    {
        printf ( "\n\n\tName : %s", cp[ i ].name ) ;
        printf ( "\n\tAge : %d", cp[ i ].age ) ;
        printf ( "\n\tNo of tests : %d", cp[ i ].notest ) ;
        printf ( "\n\tAverage : %f", cp[ i ].avgrun ) ;
    }
}
/* Function to set the values of the structure */
void setdata( )
{
    int i ;
    for ( i = 0 ; i < 3 ; i++ )
    {
        printf ( "\nEnter the name:" ) ;
        scanf ( "%s", &cp[ i ].name ) ;
        fflush ( stdin ) ;
        printf ( "\nEnter the age:" ) ;
        scanf ( "%d", &cp[ i ].age ) ;
        fflush ( stdin ) ;
```

```
        printf ( "\nEnter the total number of test matches played:" ) ;
        scanf ( "%d", &cp[ i ].notest ) ;
        fflush ( stdin ) ;
        printf ( "\nEnter the avgerage number of runs:\n\t" ) ;
        scanf ( "%f", &cp[ i ].avgrun ) ;
        fflush ( stdin ) ;
    }
}
```

(e) Suppose there is a structure called **employee** that holds information like employee code, name and date of joining. Write a program to create an array of structures and enter some data into it. Then ask the user to enter current date. Display the names of those employees whose tenure is greater than equal to 3 years.

*Program:*

```
/* To display the names of those employees whose tenure is
greater than equal to 3 years */
# include <stdio.h>
# include <stdlib.h>
#define NOOFEMP 5
struct date
{
    int day, month, year ;
} ;
int check_date ( struct date *dt ) ;
int main( )
{
    struct employee
    {
        int code ;
        char emp_name [ 20 ] ;
        struct date doj ;
    } ;
    struct employee emp [ NOOFEMP ] ;
    int i, chkdt ;
    struct date curr ;
    printf ( "\nEnter current date: " ) ;
    chkdt = check_date ( &curr ) ;
    if ( chkdt == 0 )
    {
```

```
        printf ( "\nImproper date entered" ) ;
        exit ( 0 ) ;
    }
    printf ( "\nEnter the info for %d employees : ", NOOFEMP ) ;
    for ( i = 0 ; i < NOOFEMP ; i++ )
    {
        fflush ( stdin ) ;
        printf ( "\nEmp %d :\nCode : ", i ) ;
        scanf ( "%d", &emp[ i ].code ) ;
        printf ( "\nName : " ) ;
        scanf ( "%s", emp[ i ].emp_name ) ;
        printf ( "\nDate of Joining (dd-mm-yyyy): " ) ;
        chkdt = check_date ( &emp[ i ].doj ) ;
        if ( chkdt == 0 )
        {
            printf ( "\nImproper date entered" ) ;
            exit ( 0 ) ;
        }
    }
    /* print names of employees whose tenure is 3 years or more */
    printf ( "\nEmployees whose tenure is 3 years or more: " ) ;
    for ( i = 0 ; i < NOOFEMP ; i++ )
    {
        if ( curr.year > emp[ i ].doj.year + 3 )
        {
            printf ( "\n%s", emp[ i ].emp_name ) ;
            break ;
        }
        else
        {
            if ( curr.year == emp[ i ].doj.year + 3 )
            {
                if ( curr.month > emp[ i ].doj.month )
                {
                    printf ( "\n%s", emp[ i ].emp_name ) ;
                }
                else
                {
                    if ( ( curr.month == emp[ i ].doj.month ) &&
                       ( curr.day >= emp[ i ].doj.day ) )
                        printf ( "\n%s", emp[ i ].emp_name ) ;
```

```
                    }
                }
            }
        }
        return 0 ;
    }
    /* Function to check the date entered */
    int check_date ( struct date *dt )
    {
        printf ( "\nEnter date (dd): " ) ;
        scanf ( "%d", &dt -> day ) ;
        printf ( "\nEnter month (mm): " ) ;
        scanf ( "%d", &dt -> month ) ;
        printf ( "\nEnter year (yyyy): " ) ;
        scanf ( "%d", &dt -> year ) ;
        if ( ( dt -> day > 31 || dt -> day < 0 ) ||
            ( dt -> month > 12 || dt -> month < 0 ) ||
            ( dt -> year > 9999 || dt -> year < 1000 ) )
        {
            return ( 0 ) ;
        }
        else
            return ( 1 ) ;
    }
```

(f) Create a structure called **library** to hold accession number, title of the book, author name, price of the book, and flag indicating whether book is issued or not. Write a menu-driven program that implements the working of a library. The menu options should be:

(1) Add book information
(2) Display book information
(3) List all books of given author
(4) List the title specified by accession number
(5) List the count of books in the library
(6) List the books in the order of accession number
(7) Exit

*Program:*

```
/* A menu driven program */
# include <stdio.h>
```

```
# include <string.h>
# include <stdlib.h>
void add_book( ) ;
void disp_book( ) ;
void disp_book_auth ( int aut_ano) ;
void sortbyano( ) ;
int sort_function ( const void *f, const void *ff ) ;
void linkfloat( ) ;
struct library
{
    char book_title [ 20 ] ;
    char author_name [ 20 ] ;
    int accno ;
    float price ;
    int flag ;
} ;
int count ;
struct library book [ 10 ] ;
int main( )
{
    int  choice ;
    while ( 1 )
    {
        printf ( "\n1. Add book information" ) ;
        printf ( "\n2. Display book information" ) ;
        printf ( "\n3. List all books of given author" ) ;
        printf ( "\n4. List the title of specified book" ) ;
        printf ( "\n5. List the count of books in the library" ) ;
        printf ( "\n6. List the books in order of accession number" ) ;
        printf ( "\n7. Exit" ) ;
        printf ( "\nYour choice? " ) ;
        scanf ( "%d", &choice ) ;
        switch ( choice )
        {
            case 1 :
                /* add book information */
                add_book( ) ;
                break ;
            case 2 :
                /* display book information */
                disp_book( ) ;
```

```
                break ;
            case 3 :
                /* list all books of given author */
                disp_book_auth ( 0 ) ;
                break ;
            case 4 :
                /* list the title of specified book */
                disp_book_auth ( 1 ) ;
                break ;
            case 5 :
                /* list the count of books in the library */
                printf ( "\nTotal number of books = %d", count ) ;
                break ;
            case 6 :
                /* list the books in the order of accession number */
                sortbyano( ) ;
                break ;
            case 7 :
                exit ( 0 ) ;
        }
    }
    return 0 ;
}
/* Function to add a new book */
void add_book( )
{
    if ( count == 9 )
    {
        printf ( "\nNo more space" ) ;
        return ;
    }
    printf ( "\nEnter the details of the book" ) ;
    printf ( "\nName of the book: " ) ;
    scanf ( "%s", book[ count ].book_title ) ;
    printf ( "\nName of the author: " ) ;
    scanf ( "%s", book[ count ].author_name ) ;
    printf ( "\nAccession number of the book: " ) ;
    scanf ( "%d", &book[ count ].accno ) ;
    printf ( "\nPrice of the book: " ) ;
    scanf ( "%f", &book[ count ].price ) ;
    printf ( "\nIssued / Not Issued ( 0/1 ) : " ) ;
```

```
    scanf ( "%d", &book[ count ].flag ) ;
    if ( ( book[ count ].flag != 0 ) && ( book[ count ].flag != 1 ) )
    {
        printf ( "\nImproper Status" ) ;
        return ;
    }
    count++ ;
    printf ( "\nBook details entered" ) ;
}
/* function to display books' info */
void disp_book( )
{
    int i ;
    printf ( "\nDetails of %d books in the library: ", count ) ;
    for ( i = 0 ; i < count ; i++ )
    {
        printf ( "\nName of the book: %s", book[ i ].book_title ) ;
        printf ( "\nName of author: %s", book[ i ].author_name ) ;
        printf ( "\nAccession number: %d", book[ i ].accno ) ;
        printf ( "\nPrice of the book: %f", book[ i ].price ) ;
        printf ( "\nStatus of the book: " ) ;
        book[ i ].flag == 0 ? printf ( "Issued" ) : printf ( "Available" )  ;
        printf ( "\n\n" ) ;
    }
}
/* Function to display books' info for a given author */
void disp_book_auth ( int aut_ano )
{
    char nm [ 20 ] ;
    int accno;
    int i = 0 ;
    int dec = 0 ;
    /* check if author name is given or accession no is given */
    if ( aut_ano == 0 )
    {
        printf ( "\nEnter the name of the author : " ) ;
        scanf ( "%s", nm ) ;
        printf ( "\nDetails of books by author %s in library: ", nm ) ;
    }
    else
    {
```

```
        printf ( "\nEnter the accession number of the book : " ) ;
        scanf ( "%d", &accno ) ;
        printf ( "\nDetails of books with accession no %d: ", accno ) ;
    }
    for ( i = 0 ; i < count ; i++ )
    {
        if ( ( strcmp ( nm, book[ i ].author_name ) == 0 ) &&
            ( aut_ano == 0 ) )
            dec++ ;
        else
        {
            if ( aut_ano == 1 )
            {
                if ( book[ i ].accno == accno )
                    dec++ ;
                else
                    continue ;
            }
            else
                break ;
        }
        printf ( "\nName of the book: %s", book[ i ].book_title ) ;
        printf ( "\nName of author: %s", book[ i ].author_name ) ;
        printf ( "\nAccession num of book: %d", book[ i ].accno ) ;
        printf ( "\nPrice of the book: %f", book[ i ].price ) ;
        printf ( "\nStatus of the book: " ) ;
        book[ i ].flag == 0 ? printf ( "Issued" ) : printf ( "Available" ) ;
        printf ( "\n\n" ) ;
    }
    if ( dec == 0 )
        printf ( "\nNo such book" ) ;
}
/* Function to sot books by accession number */
void sortbyano( )
{
    qsort ( ( struct library * ) book, count, sizeof ( book[ 0 ] ),
            sort_function ) ;
    printf ( "\nAfter sorting by accession number " ) ;
    disp_book ( ) ;
}
int sort_function ( const void *f, const void *ff )
```

```
{
    return ( ( ( struct library *) f ) -> accno -
              ( ( struct library * ) ff ) -> accno ) ;
}
void linkfloat( )
{
    float a = 0, *b ;
    b = &a ;
    a = *b ;
}
```

(g) Define a function that compares two given dates. To store a date, use a structure that contains three members namely day, month and year. If the dates are equal the function should return 0, otherwise it should return 1.

*Program:*

```
/* Create Date structure and compare the dates */
# include <stdio.h>
# include <stdlib.h>
struct date
{
    int day, month, year ;
} ;
int check_date ( struct date *dt ) ;
int main( )
{
    int chkdt ;
    struct date d1, d2 ;
    /* input the dates to be compared */
    printf ( "\nEnter the dates to be compared: " ) ;
    chkdt = check_date ( &d1 ) ;
    if ( chkdt == 0 )
        exit ( 0 ) ;
    fflush ( stdin ) ;
    chkdt = check_date ( &d2 ) ;
    if ( chkdt == 0 )
        exit ( 0 ) ;
    /*Compare the two structures*/
    if ( ( d1.day == d2.day ) && ( d1.month == d2.month )
        && ( d1.year == d2.year ) )
```

```
        printf ( "\nDates are Equal" ) ;
    else
        printf ( "\nDates are Unequal" ) ;
    return 0 ;
}
/* Function to check the date entered */
int check_date ( struct date *dt )
{
    printf ( "\nEnter date (dd): " ) ;
    scanf ( "%d", &dt -> day ) ;
    printf ( "\nEnter month (mm): " ) ;
    scanf ( "%d", &dt -> month ) ;
    printf ( "\nEnter year (yyyy): " ) ;
    scanf ( "%d", &dt -> year ) ;
    if ( ( dt -> day > 31 || dt -> day < 0 ) ||
        ( dt -> month > 12 || dt -> month < 0 ) ||
        ( dt -> year > 9999 || dt -> year < 1000 ) )
    {
        printf ( "\nImproper date entered" ) ;
        return ( 0 ) ;
    }
    else
        return ( 1 ) ;
}
```

**CHAPTER**

# EIGHTEEN

# Console Input/Output

**[A]** What will be the output of the following programs?

(a)
```
# include <stdio.h>
# include <ctype.h>
int main( )
{
    char ch ;
    ch = getchar( ) ;
    if ( islower ( ch ) )
        putchar ( toupper ( ch ) ) ;
    else
        putchar ( tolower ( ch ) ) ;
    return 0 ;
}
```

| *Input* | *Output:* |
|---|---|
| a | A |
| Z | z |

(b)
```
# include <stdio.h>
int main( )
{
    int i = 2 ;
    float f = 2.5367 ;
    char str[ ] = "Life is like that" ;
    printf ( "%4d\t%3.3f\t%4s\n", i, f, str ) ;
    return 0 ;
}
```

*Output:*

```
2    2.537   Life is like that
```

(c)
```
# include <stdio.h>
int main( )
{
    printf ( "More often than \b\b not \rthe person who \
            wins is the one who thinks he can!\n" ) ;
    return 0 ;
}
```

*Output:*

```
the person who                 wins is the one who thinks he can!
```

(d)
```
# include <conio.h>
char  p[ ] = "The sixth sick sheikh's sixth ship is sick" ;
int main( )
{
    int  i = 0 ;
    while ( p[ i ] != '\0' )
    {
        putchar ( p[ i ] ) ;
        i++ ;
    }
    return 0 ;
}
```

*Output:*

```
The sixth sick sheikh's sixth ship is sick
```

**[B]** Point out the errors, if any, in the following programs:

(a)
```
# include <stdio.h>
int main( )
{
    int i ;
    char a[ ] = "Hello" ;
    while ( a != '\0' )
    {
        printf ( "%c", *a ) ;
        a++ ;
```

```
    }
    return 0 ;
}
```

Error. Lvalue required. Post-fix increment operator cannot be used with the name of the array.

(b)
```
# include <stdio.h >
int main( )
{
    double dval ;
    scanf ( "%f", &dval ) ;
    printf ( "Double Value = %lf\n", dval ) ;
    return 0 ;
}
```

No Error. But the format specifier used for **double** in **scanf( )** should be **lf** instead of **f**.

(c)
```
# include <stdio.h>
int main( )
{
    int ival ;
    scanf ( "%d\n", &n ) ;
    printf ( "Integer Value = %d\n", ival ) ;
    return 0 ;
}
```

Error. Undefined symbol **n**.

(d)
```
# include <stdio.h>
int main( )
{
    int dd, mm, yy ;
    printf ( "Enter day, month and year\n" ) ;
    scanf ( "%d%*c%d%*c%d", &dd, &mm, &yy ) ;
    printf ( "The date is: %d - %d - %d\n", dd, mm, yy ) ;
    return 0 ;
}
```

No Error. The asterisk (*) acts as a suppression character. Giving '*' in **scanf( )** would skip the assignment of next scanned value to the specified address..

(e)
```
# include <stdio.h>
int main( )
{
    char text ;
    sprintf ( text, "%4d\t%2.2f\n%s", 12, 3.452, "Merry Go Round" ) ;
    printf ( "%s\n", text ) ;
    return 0 ;
}
```

Error. **text** must be char *.

(f)
```
# include <stdio.h>
int main( )
{
    char buffer[ 50 ] ;
    int no = 97;
    double val = 2.34174 ;
    char name[ 10 ] = "Shweta" ;
    sprintf ( buffer, "%d %lf %s", no, val, name ) ;
    printf ( "%s\n", buffer ) ;
    sscanf ( buffer, "%4d %2.2lf %s", &no, &val, name ) ;
    printf ( "%s\n", buffer ) ;
    printf ( "%d %lf %s\n", no, val, name ) ;
    return 0 ;
}
```

No error.

**[C]** Answer the following:

(a) To receive the string "We have got the guts, you get the glory!!" in an array **char str[ 100 ]** which of the following functions would you use?

1. scanf ( "%s", str ) ;
2. gets ( str ) ;
3. getche ( str ) ;
4. fgetchar ( str ) ;

*Answer:*

2. gets( )

(b) If an integer is to be entered through the keyboard, which function would you use?

1. scanf( )
2. gets( )
3. getche( )
4. getchar( )

*Answer:*

1. scanf( )

(c) Which of the following can a format string of a **printf( )** function contain:

1. Characters, format specifications and escape sequences
2. Characters, integers and floats
3. Strings, integers and escape sequences
4. Inverted commas, percentage sign and backslash character

*Answer:*

1. Characters, conversion specifications and escape sequences

(d) The purpose of the field-width specifier in a **printf( )** function is to:

1. Control the margins of the program listing
2. Specify the maximum value of a number
3. Control the size of font used to print numbers
4. Specify how many columns should be used to print the number

*Answer:*

4. Specifies how many columns will be used to print the number

(e) If we are to display the following output properly aligned which format specifiers would you use?

| | | |
|---|---|---|
| Discovery of India | Jawaharlal Nehru | 425.50 |
| My Experiments with Truth | Mahatma Gandhi | 375.50 |
| Sunny Days | Sunil Gavaskar | 95.50 |
| One More Over | Erapalli Prasanna | 85.00 |

*Program:*

```
#include <stdio.h>
int main( )
```

```
{
    printf ( "%-30s%-20s%-10.2f\n", "Discovery of India",
            "Jawaharlal Nehru", 425.50 ) ;
    printf ( "%-30s%-20s%-10.2f\n", "My Experiments with Truth",
            "Mahatma Gandhi", 375.50 ) ;
    printf ( "%-30s%-20s%-10.2f\n", "Sunny Days",
            "Sunil Gavaskar", 95.50 ) ;
    printf ( "%-30s%-20s%-10.2f\n", "One More Over",
            "Erapalli Prasanna", 85.00 ) ;
    return 0 ;
}
```

# CHAPTER NINETEEN

# File Input/Output

**[A]** Answer the following questions:

(a) In which file FILE structure is defined?

*Answer:*

stdio.h

(b) If a file contains the line "I am a boy\r\n" then on reading this line into the array **str[ ]** using **fgets( )** what would **str[ ]** contain?

*Answer:*

I am a boy\r\n\0

(c) State True or False:

1. The disadvantage of high-level file I/O functions is that the programmer has to manage the file buffers.

   Answer: False

2. If a file is opened for reading, it is necessary that the file must exist.

   Answer: True

3. If a file opened for writing already exists, its contents would be overwritten.

   Answer: True

4. For opening a file in append mode it is necessary that the file should exist.

Answer: False

(d) On opening a file for reading which of the following activities are performed:

1. The disk is searched for existence of the file.
2. The file contents are brought into memory.
3. A pointer is set up which points to the first character in the file.
4. All the above.

*Answer:*

4. All the above

(e) Is it necessary that a file created in text mode must always be opened in text mode for subsequent operations?

*Answer:*

Yes

**[B]** Attempt the following questions:

(a) Suppose a file contains student records with each record containing name and age of a student. Write a program to read these records and display them in sorted order by name.

*Program:*

```
# include <stdio.h>
# include <string.h>
int main( )
{
    FILE *fp ;
    struct stud
    {
        char name[ 40 ] ;
        int age ;
    } ;
    struct stud s, stud[ 10 ], temp ;
    int n, j, k, ii ;
    fp = fopen ( "STUDENT.DAT", "rb" ) ;
```

```
    n = 0 ;
    while ( fread ( &s, sizeof ( s ), 1, fp ) == 1 )
    {
        stud[ n ] = s ;
        n++ ;
    }
    for ( j = 0 ; j < n - 1 ; j++ )
    {
        for ( k = j + 1 ; k < n ; k++ )
        {
            if ( strcmp ( stud[ j ].name, stud[ k ].name ) > 0 )
            {
                temp = stud[ j ] ;
                stud[ j ] = stud[ k ] ;
                stud[ k ] = temp ;
            }
        }
    }
    fclose ( fp ) ;
    for ( j = 0 ; j < n ; j++ )
        printf ( "Name: %s age: %d\n", stud[ j ].name, stud[ j ].age );
    return 0 ;
}
```

(b) Write a program to copy contents of one file to another. While doing so replace all lowercase characters to their equivalent uppercase characters.

*Program:*

```
/* Program to copy one text file to another and replace all
lowercase characters to uppercase */
# include <stdio.h>
# include <stdlib.h>
# include <ctype.h>  /* for prototypes of islower( ), toupper( ) */
int main( )
{
    FILE *fs, *ft ;
    char ch ;
    char  source[ 67 ], target[ 67 ] ;
    puts ( "Enter source file name: " ) ;
```

```
    gets ( source ) ;
    puts ( "Enter target file name: " ) ;
    gets ( target ) ;
    fs = fopen ( source, "r" ) ;
    if ( fs == NULL )
    {
        puts ( "Unable to open source file" ) ;
        exit ( 0 ) ;
    }
    ft = fopen ( target, "w" ) ;
    if ( ft == NULL )
    {
        fclose ( fs ) ;
        puts ( "Unable to open target file" ) ;
        exit ( 0 ) ;
    }
    while ( ( ch = fgetc ( fs ) ) != EOF )
    {
        if ( islower ( ch ) )
            fputc ( toupper ( ch ), ft ) ;
        else
            fputc ( ch, ft ) ;
    }
    printf ( "\nFile copied!!\n" ) ;
    fclose ( fs ) ;
    fclose ( ft ) ;
    return 0 ;
}
```

(c) Write a program that merges lines alternately from two files and writes the results to a new file. If one file has a smaller number of lines than the other, the remaining lines from the larger file should be simply copied into the target file.

*Program:*

```
/* Copy the contents of two files alternatively in a new text file */
# include <stdio.h>
# include <string.h>
int main( )
{
```

```
FILE *fs1, *fs2, *ft ;
char  str1[ 80 ], str2[ 80 ] ;
char  source1[ 67 ], source2[ 67 ], target[ 67 ] ;
char *ptrch, newl = '\n' ;
int flag = 0 ;
puts ( "Enter source1 file name: " ) ;
gets ( source1 ) ;
puts ( "Enter source2 file name: " ) ;
gets ( source2 ) ;
puts ( "Enter target file name: " ) ;
gets ( target ) ;
fs1 = fopen ( source1, "r" ) ;
if ( fs1 == NULL )
{
    puts ( "Unable to open source1" ) ;
    exit ( 0 ) ;
}
fs2 = fopen ( source2, "r" ) ;
if ( fs2 == NULL )
{
    puts ( "Unable to open source2" ) ;
    fclose ( fs2 ) ;
    exit ( 0 ) ;
}
ft = fopen ( target, "w+" ) ;
if ( ft == NULL )
{
    fclose ( fs1 ) ;
    fclose ( fs2 ) ;
    puts ( "Unable to create target file" ) ;
    exit ( 0 ) ;
}
/* read the source files and copy the strings alternately */
/* read till the eof of any one of the files is reached */
while ( fgets ( str1, 79, fs1 ) != NULL )
{
    ptrch = strchr ( str1, newl ) ;
    fputs ( str1, ft ) ;
    if ( !ptrch )
        fputs ( "\n", ft ) ;
    if ( fgets ( str2, 79, fs2 ) != NULL )
```

```
            {
                fputs ( str2, ft ) ;
                ptrch = strchr ( str2, newl ) ;
                flag = 1 ;
                if ( !ptrch )
                    fputs ( "\n", ft ) ;
            }
            else
                fputs ( "\n", ft ) ;
        }
        /* copy the contents of the file whose eof is not reached */
        if ( flag == 1 )
        {
            while ( fgets ( str2, 79, fs2 ) != NULL )
            {
                ptrch = strchr ( str1, newl ) ;
                fputs ( str2, ft ) ;
                if ( ptrch )
                    fputs ( "\n", ft ) ;
            }
        }
        printf ( "\nCopying files completed!!\n" ) ;
        fclose ( fs1 ) ;
        fclose ( fs2 ) ;
        fclose ( ft ) ;
        return 0 ;
    }
```

(d) Write a program to encrypt/decrypt a file using:

(1) Offset cipher: In an offset cipher each character from the source file is offset with a fixed value and then written to the target file.

For example, if character read from the source file is 'A', then convert this into a new character by offsetting 'A' by a fixed value, say 128, and then writing the new character to the target file.

*Program:*

```
/* Encrypt / Decrypt a file using offset cipher */
```

```
# include <stdio.h>
FILE  *fs ,*ft ;
void code( ) ;
void decode( ) ;
int main ( int  argc, char  *argv[   ] )
{
    if ( argc != 4 )
    {
        puts ( "Improper usage. Correct usage is:\n" ) ;
        puts ( "CH11GF1 <source file> <target file> <C/D>\n" ) ;
        exit ( 1 ) ;
    }
    fs = fopen ( argv[ 1 ], "r" ) ;
    if ( fs == NULL )
    {
        printf ( "Cannot open source file\n" ) ;
        puts ( argv[ 1 ] ) ;
        exit ( 2 ) ;
    }
    ft = fopen ( argv[ 2 ], "w" ) ;
    if ( ft == NULL )
    {
        puts ( "Cannot open target file\n" ) ;
        puts ( argv[ 2 ] ) ;
        fclose ( fs ) ;
        exit ( 3 ) ;
    }
    if ( *argv[ 3 ] == 'c' || *argv[ 3 ] == 'C' )
        code( ) ;
    else
        decode( ) ;
    fclose ( fs ) ;
    fclose ( ft ) ;
    printf ( "Mission Accomplished\n" ) ;
    return 0 ;
}
void code( )
{
    int  ch ;
    while ( ( ch = getc ( fs ) ) !=  EOF )
    {
```

```
            ch = ch + 128 ;  /* encrypt  */
            putc ( ch, ft ) ;
        }
    }
    void decode( )
    {
        int  ch ;
        while ( ( ch = getc ( fs ) ) != EOF )
        {
            ch = ch - 128 ;  /* decrypt */
            putc ( ch, ft ) ;
        }
    }
```

(2) Substitution cipher: In this cipher for each character read from the source file a corresponding predetermined character is written to the target file.

For example, if character 'A' is read from the source file, and if we have decided that every 'A' is to be substituted by '!', then a '!' would be written to the target file in place of every 'A'. Similarly, every 'B' would be substituted by '5' and so on.

*Program:*

```
/* Encrypt / Decrypt a file using substitution cipher */
/ * Type the strings in arr1 and arr2 very meticulously */
# include <stdio.h>
# include <stdlib.h>
FILE  *fs, *ft ;
void code( ) ;
void decode( ) ;
int main ( int  argc, char  *argv[  ] )
{
    if ( argc != 4 )
    {
        puts ( "Improper usage. Correct usage is:\n" ) ;
        puts ( "CH19Bd2 <source file> <target file> C/D\n" ) ;
        exit ( 1 ) ;
    }
    fs = fopen ( argv[ 1 ], "r" ) ;
    if ( fs == NULL )
```

```
    {
        puts ( "Cannot open source file\n" ) ;
        exit ( 2 ) ;
    }
    ft = fopen ( argv[ 2 ], "w" ) ;
    if ( ft == NULL )
    {
        puts ( "Cannot open target file\n" ) ;
        fclose ( fs ) ;
        exit ( 3 ) ;
    }
    if ( *argv[ 3 ] == 'c' || *argv[ 3 ] == 'C' )
        code( ) ;
    else
    {
        if ( *argv[ 3 ] == 'd' || *argv[ 3 ] == 'D' )
            decode( ) ;
        else
        {
            fclose ( fs ) ;
            fclose ( ft ) ;
            puts ( "Improper usage\n" ) ;
            exit ( 4 ) ;
        }
    }
    fclose ( fs ) ;
    fclose ( ft ) ;

    return 0 ;
}
void code( )
{
    char ch ;
    int i = 0 ;
    char arr1[ 97 ] = " IOP{}asdfghjkl;'ASDFGHJKL:zxcvbnm,./
ZXCVBNM<>?`1234567890-=\~!@#$%^&*()_+|qwertyuiop[]
QWERTYU" ;
    char arr2[ 97 ] = " `1234567890-=\~!@#$%^&*()_+|qwert
yuiop[]QWERTYUIOP{}asdfghjkl;'ASDFGHJKL:zxcvbnm,./ZXCV
BNM<>?" ;
```

```
    arr2[ 93 ] = '\\' ;
    arr1[ 93 ] = '\\' ;
    arr2[ 94 ] = '\"' ;
    arr1[ 94 ] = '\"' ;
    arr2[ 95 ] = '\n' ;
    arr1[ 95 ] = '\n' ;
    arr1[ 96 ] = '\t';
    arr2[ 96 ] = '\t' ;
    while ( ( ch = getc ( fs ) ) != EOF )
    {
        for ( i = 0 ; i <= 96 ; i++ )
        {
            if ( ch == arr1[ i ] )
                break ;
        }
        putc ( arr2[ i ], ft ) ;
    }
}
void decode( )
{
    char  ch ;
    int  i = 0 ;
    char  arr1[ 97 ] = " `1234567890-=\~!@#$%^&*()_+|qwert
yuiop[]QWERTYUIOP{}asdfghjkl;'ASDFGHJKL:zxcvbnm,./ZXCV
BNM<>?" ;
    char  arr2[ 97 ] = " IOP{}asdfghjkl;'ASDFGHJKL:zxcvbnm,./
ZXCVBNM<>?`1234567890-=\~!@#$%^&*()_+|qwertyuiop[]
QWERTYU" ;
    arr1[ 93 ] = '\\' ;
    arr2[ 94 ] = '\"' ;
    arr1[ 94 ] = '\"' ;
    arr2[ 95 ] = '\n' ;
    arr1[ 95 ] = '\n' ;
    arr1[ 96 ] = '\t';
    arr2[ 96 ] = '\t' ;
    while ( ( ch = getc ( fs ) ) != EOF )
    {
        for ( i = 0 ; i <= 96 ; i++ )
        {
            if ( ch == arr2[ i ] )
```

```
                break ;
            }
            putc ( arr1[ i ], ft ) ;
        }
    }
```

(e) In the file 'CUSTOMER.DAT' there are 10 records with the following structure:

```
struct customer
{
    int  accno ;
    char name[ 30 ] ;
    float  balance ;
} ;
```

In another file 'TRANSACTIONS.DAT' there are several records with the following structure:

```
struct trans
{
    int  accno ;
    char trans_type ;
    float amount ;
} ;
```

The element **trans_type** contains D/W indicating deposit or withdrawal of amount. Write a program to update 'CUSTOMER.DAT' file, i.e. if the **trans_type** is 'D' then update the **balance** of 'CUSTOMER.DAT' by adding **amount** to balance for the corresponding **accno**. Similarly, if **trans_type** is 'W' then subtract the **amount** from **balance**. However, while subtracting the amount ensure that the amount should not get overdrawn, i.e. at least 100 Rs. should remain in the account.

*Program:*

```
/* To copy a field from a data file to another data file */
# include <stdio.h>
# include <stdlib.h>
struct customer
{
    int  accno ;
```

```
    char name[ 30 ] ;
    float  balance ;
} ;
struct trans
{
    int  accno ;
    char trans_type ;
    float amount ;

} ;

int main( )
{
    struct customer s ;
    struct trans ss ;
    FILE  *fs , *ft ;
    int  slen = sizeof ( struct customer ) ;
    fs = fopen ( "TRANSACTION.DAT", "rb" ) ;
    if ( fs == NULL )
    {
        puts ( "Cannot open file: TRANSACTION.DAT\n" ) ;
        exit ( 1 ) ;
    }
    ft = fopen ( "CUSTOMER.DAT", "rb+" ) ;
    if ( ft == NULL )
    {
        puts ( "Cannot open file: CUSTOMER.DAT\n" ) ;
        fclose ( fs ) ;
        exit ( 2 ) ;
    }
    while ( fread ( &ss, sizeof ( ss ), 1, fs ) == 1 )
    {
        fseek ( ft, 0, SEEK_SET ) ;
        while ( fread ( &s, slen, 1, ft ) == 1 )
        {
            if ( s.accno == ss.accno )
            {
                if ( ss.trans_type == 'D' )
                    s.balance += ss.amount ;
                else
                {
                    if ( ( ss.trans_type == 'W' ) &&
```

```
                        ( s.balance - ss.amount > 100 ) )
                    s.balance -= ss.amount ;
                else
                    s.balance = 100 ;
            }
            fseek ( ft, -slen, SEEK_CUR ) ;
            fwrite ( &s, slen, 1, ft ) ;
            break ;
        }
    }
}
fclose ( fs ) ;
fclose ( ft ) ;
return 0 ;
}
```

(f) There are 10 records present in a file with the following structure:

```
struct date
{
    int d, m, y ;
} ;
struct employee
{
    int  empcode[ 6 ] ;
    char empname[ 20 ] ;
    struct date join_date ;
    float salary ;
} ;
```

Write a program to read these records, arrange them in ascending order by **join_date** and write them to a target file.

*Program:*

```
/* To arrange records in a file in ascending order of joining date */
# include <stdio.h>
# include <stdlib.h>
struct date
{
    int d, m, y ;
} ;
```

```
int isgreater ( struct date, struct date ) ;
int main( )
{
    struct employee
    {
        int  empcode[ 6 ] ;
        char empname[ 20 ] ;
        struct date join_date ;
        float salary ;
    } ;
    struct employee emp[ 100 ], s, temp  ;
    int j, k ;
    FILE *fs, *ft ;
    int n ;
    fs = fopen ( "EMP.DAT", "rb" ) ;
    if ( fs == NULL )
    {
        puts ( "Cannot open file: EMP.DAT\n" ) ;
        exit ( 1 ) ;
    }
    ft = fopen ( "ASCEMP.DAT", "wb" ) ;
    if ( ft == NULL )
    {
        puts ( "Cannot open file: ASCEMP.DAT\n" ) ;
        fclose ( fs ) ;
        exit ( 2 ) ;
    }
    n = 0 ;
    while ( fread ( &s, sizeof( s ), 1, fs ) == 1 )
    {
        emp[ n ] = s ;
        n++ ;
    }
    for ( j = 0 ; j < n - 1 ; j++ )
    {
        for ( k = j + 1 ; k < n ; k++ )
        {
            if ( isgreater ( emp[ j ].join_date, emp[ k ].join_date ))
            {
                temp = emp[ j ] ;
                emp[ j ] = emp[ k ] ;
```

```
                emp[ k ] = temp ;
            }
        }
    }
    for ( j = 0 ; j < n ; j++ )
        fwrite ( &emp[ j ], sizeof ( s ), 1, ft ) ;
    fclose ( fs ) ;
    fclose ( ft ) ;
    printf ( "Records arranged in ascending order\n" ) ;
    return 0 ;
}
int isgreater ( struct date d1, struct date d2 )
{
    if ( d1.y > d2.y )
        return ( 1 ) ;
    else
    {
        if ( d1.y == d2.y )
        {
            if ( d1.m > d2.m )
                return ( 1 ) ;
            else
            {
                if ( ( d1.m == d2.m ) && ( d1.d >= d2.d ) )
                    return ( 1 ) ;
            }
        }
    }
    return 0 ;
}
```

(g) A hospital keeps a file of blood donors in which each record has the format:

Name: 20 columns
Address: 40 columns
Age: 2 columns
Blood Type: 1 column (Type 1, 2, 3 or 4)
Write a program to read the file and print a list of all blood donors whose age is below 25 and whose blood type is 2.

*Program:*

```
/* To Read file in binary mode and display its contents */
# include <stdio.h>
int main( )
{
    struct donors
    {
        char  name[ 21 ] ;
        char  address[ 41 ] ;
        int  age ;
        char  bloodtype ;
    } ;
    struct donors hospital ;
    FILE *fp ;
    fp = fopen ( "hospital.dat", "rb" ) ;
    if ( fp == NULL )
    {
        puts ( "Cannot open file\n" ) ;
        exit ( 1 ) ;
    }
    while ( fread ( &hospital, sizeof ( hospital ), 1, fp ) == 1 )
    {
        if ( hospital.age < 25 && hospital.bloodtype == '2' )
            printf ( "%s %s %d %c\n", hospital.name,
                hospital.address, hospital.age, hospital.bloodtype ) ;
    }
    fclose ( fp ) ;
    return 0 ;
}
```

In order to run this program, you must have a file "Hospital.dat". If you do not have such a file, you can use the following code to create this file with 5 records.

```
# include <stdio.h>
# include <stdlib.h>
int main( )
{
    struct donors
    {
```

```
        char name[ 21 ] ;
        char address[ 41 ] ;
        int age ;
        char bloodtype ;
    } ;
    struct donors hospital ;
    int i ;
    FILE *fp ;
    fp = fopen ( "hospital.dat", "wb" ) ;
    if ( fp == NULL )
    {
        puts ( "Cannot open file\n" ) ;
        exit ( 1 ) ;
    }
    for ( i = 0 ; i < 5 ; i ++ )
    {
        printf ( "\nName: " ) ;
        scanf ( "%s", hospital.name ) ;
        fflush ( stdin ) ;
        printf ( "\nAddress: " ) ;
        scanf ( "%s", hospital.address ) ;
        fflush ( stdin ) ;
        printf ( "\nAge: " ) ;
        scanf ( "%d", &hospital.age ) ;
        fflush ( stdin ) ;
        printf ( "\nType: " ) ;
        scanf ( "%c", &hospital.bloodtype ) ;
        fflush ( stdin ) ;
        fwrite ( &hospital, sizeof ( hospital ), 1, fp ) ;
    }
    fcloseall ( ) ;
    return 0 ;
}
```

(h) Given a list of names of students in a class, write a program to store the names in a file on disk. Make a provision to display the **n**th name in the list, where **n** is read from the keyboard.

*Program:*

```
/* Create a file on disk, retrieve data as required */
```

```
# include <stdio.h>
int main( )
{
    FILE *fp ;
    char  name[ 21 ], ch, another = 'y' ;
    int  num, n ;

    fp = fopen ( "student.dat", "w+" ) ;
    if ( fp == NULL )
    {
        puts ( "Unable to create file\n" ) ;
        exit ( 1 ) ;
    }
    /* Loop for data entry */
    while ( another == 'y' || another == 'Y' )
    {
        puts ( "\nEnter the name of student: " ) ;
        gets ( name ) ;
        fputs ( name, fp ) ;  /* write data to file */
        fputs ( "\n", fp ) ;  /* add newline character at the end
                                 of record */
        puts ( "Do you want to add more names y/n" ) ;
        fflush ( stdin ) ;
        another = getch( ) ;
    }
    fseek ( fp, 0L, SEEK_SET ) ;  /* File pointer reset to start of file */
    puts ( "\nEnter any number from the list" ) ;
    scanf ( "%d", &num ) ;
    n = num ;
    while ( fgets ( name, 21, fp ) != NULL )
    {
        num-- ;  /* count downwords to reach the required record */
        if ( num == 0 )
            printf ( "\nName of student no. %d is: %s\n", n, name ) ;
    }
    if ( num > 0 )
        puts ( "No such number exists in the list\n" ) ;
    fseek ( fp, 0L, SEEK_SET ) ;  /* reset file pointer */
    puts ( "\nList of students whose name starts with S: " ) ;
    while ( fgets ( name, 21, fp ) != NULL )
    {
```

```
        if ( name[ 0 ] == 's' || name[ 0 ] == 'S' )
            printf ( "%s", name ) ;
    }
    fclose ( fp ) ;
    return 0 ;
}
```

(i) Assume that a Master file contains two fields—roll number and name of the student. At the end of the year, a set of students join the class and another set leaves. A Transaction file contains the roll numbers and an appropriate code to add or delete a student.

Write a program to create another file that contains the updated list of names and roll numbers. Assume that the Master file and the Transaction file are arranged in ascending order by roll numbers. The updated file should also be in ascending order by roll numbers.

*Program:*

```
/* Create an updated file from Master & Transaction File */
# include <stdio.h>
# include <stdlib.h>
int main( )
{
    FILE *mf, *tf, *uf ;
    struct master  /* Master file structure */
    {
        int  rollno ;
        char  name[ 20 ] ;
    } ;
    struct transaction  /* Transaction file structure */
    {
        char  code ;
        int  rollup ;
        char  name1[ 20 ] ;
    } ;
    struct master student, newstudent ;
    struct transaction add_del ;
    int  msz = sizeof ( struct master ) ;
    mf = fopen ( "master.dat", "r" ) ;
    if ( mf == NULL )
    {
```

```
        puts ( "Unable to open master file\n" ) ;
        exit ( 1 ) ;
    }
    tf = fopen ( "transact.dat", "r" ) ;
    if ( tf == NULL )
    {
        puts ( "Unable to open transaction file\n" ) ;
        fclose ( mf ) ;
        exit ( 2 ) ;
    }
    uf = fopen ( "updated.dat", "w+" ) ;
    if ( uf == NULL )
    {
        puts ( "Unable to create updated file\n" ) ;
        fclose ( mf ) ;
        fclose ( tf ) ;
        exit ( 3 ) ;
    }
    while ( fread ( &add_del, sizeof ( struct transaction ), 1, tf ) == 1 )
    {
        fread ( &student, msz, 1, mf ) ;
        /* if code = d, don't do anything */
        if ( add_del.code == 'd' )
        {
            if ( student.rollno == add_del.rollup )
                continue ;
            else
            {
                /* code != d, write to updated file from master file */
                while ( student.rollno != add_del.rollup )
                {
                    fwrite ( &student, msz, 1, uf ) ;
                    fread ( &student, msz, 1, mf ) ;
                }
            }
            continue ;
        }
        /* write all records from master file to updated file where
           roll no of master file < roll no of transaction file */
        while ( student.rollno < add_del.rollup )
        {
```

```
            fwrite ( &student, msz, 1, uf ) ;
            fread ( &student, msz, 1, mf ) ;
        }
        /* copy record from transaction file to updated file where
           code != d ( new student has to be added ) */
        newstudent.rollno = add_del.rollup ;
        strcpy ( newstudent.name, add_del.name1 ) ;
        fwrite ( &newstudent, msz, 1, uf ) ;
        fseek ( mf,-msz, SEEK_CUR ) ;
    } /* end of while loop */
    /* write rest of the records from master file to updated file for
        which there is no matching record in transaction file */
    while ( fread ( &student, msz, 1, mf ) == 1 )
        fwrite ( &student, msz, 1, uf ) ;
    fclose ( mf ) ;
    fclose ( tf ) ;
    fclose ( uf ) ;
    printf ( "Updated file saved\n" ) ;
    return 0 ;
}
```

The "master.dat" and "transact.dat" file can be created using the following code. Pl. ensure that your directory is correctly set.

```
# include <stdio.h>
# include <stdlib.h>
int main( )
{
    FILE *mf, *tf, *uf ;
    struct master
    {
        int  rollno ;
        char  name[ 20 ] ;
    } ;
    struct transaction
    {
        char  code ;
        int  rollup ;
        char  name1[ 20 ] ;
    } ;
    struct master student, newstudent ;
```

```
struct transaction add_del ;
int  i, msz = sizeof ( struct master ) ;
mf = fopen ( "master.dat", "w" ) ;
if ( mf == NULL )
{
    puts ( "Unable to open master file\n" ) ;
    exit ( 1 ) ;
}
for ( i =  0 ; i <= 2 ; i++ )
{
    printf ( "\nRollno: " ) ;
    scanf ( "%d", &student.rollno ) ;
    fflush ( stdin ) ;
    printf ( "\nName: " ) ;
    scanf ( "%s", &student.name ) ;
    fflush ( stdin ) ;
    fwrite ( &student, sizeof ( student ), 1, mf ) ;
}
fcloseall( ) ;

tf = fopen ( "transact.dat", "w" ) ;

if ( tf == NULL )
{
    puts ( "Unable to open master file\n" ) ;
    exit ( 2 ) ;
}
for ( i =  0 ; i <= 1 ; i++ )
{
    printf ( "\nCode: " ) ;
    scanf ( "%c", &add_del.code ) ;
    fflush ( stdin ) ;
    printf ( "\nRollno: " ) ;
    scanf ( "%d", &add_del.rollup ) ;
    fflush ( stdin ) ;
    printf ( "\nName: " ) ;
    scanf ( "%s", &add_del.name1 ) ;
    fflush ( stdin ) ;
    fwrite ( &add_del, sizeof ( add_del ), 1, tf ) ;
}
fcloseall( ) ;
```

```
    return 0 ;
}
```

(j) Given a text file, write a program to create another text file deleting the words “a”, “the”, “an” and replacing each one of them with a blank space.

*Program:*

```
/* Create a new text file after replacing "a", "an" & "the" with a
blank space from a given text file */
# include <stdio.h>
# include <stdlib.h>
# include <string.h>
FILE *ft ;
int charcount ;
void newstr ( char *, char * ) ;
int main( )
{
    FILE *fs ;
    char str[ 80 ], source[ 67 ], target[ 67 ] ;
    char *apstr[ ] = { "a", "the", "an" } ;
    int i ;
    puts ( "Enter source file name: " ) ;
    gets ( source ) ;
    puts ( "Enter target file name: " ) ;
    gets ( target ) ;
    fs = fopen ( source, "r" ) ; /* read only mode for source file */
    if ( fs == NULL )
    {
        puts ( "Unable to open source file\n" ) ;
        exit ( 1 ) ;
    }
    ft = fopen ( target, "w+" ) ;
    if ( ft == NULL )
    {
        fclose ( fs ) ;
        puts ( "Unable to create target file\n" ) ;
        exit ( 2 ) ;
    }
    while ( fgets ( str, 79, fs ) != NULL )
```

```
    {
        newstr ( str, apstr[ 0 ] ) ;
        for ( i = 1 ; i <= 2 ; i++ )
        {
            fseek ( ft, -charcount, SEEK_CUR ) ;
            fgets ( str, charcount, ft ) ;
            fseek ( ft, -charcount, SEEK_CUR ) ;
            newstr ( str, apstr[ i ] ) ;
        }
    }
    fclose ( fs ) ;
    fclose ( ft ) ;
    return 0 ;
}
void newstr ( char  *p, char  *t )
{
    int  len = strlen ( t ) ;
    charcount = 0 ;
    while ( *p )
    {
        if ( ( !strncmp ( p, t, len ) && ( *( p - 1 ) == ' ' ) && ( *( p + len )
          == ' ' ||  *( p + len )  == '\n' ) ) || ( !strncmp ( p, t, len ) && (
         charcount == 0 ) &&
            ( *( p + len ) == ' ' || *( p + len )  == '\n' ) ) )
        {
            fputc ( ' ', ft ) ;
            p = p + strlen ( t ) - 1 ;
        }
        else
            fputc ( *p, ft ) ;
        p++ ;
        charcount++ ;
    }
    charcount++ ;
}
```

# CHAPTER TWENTY

# More Issues In Input/Output

[A] Answer the following questions:

(a) How will you use the program given below to perform the following operations?

- Copy the contents of one file into another.
- Create a new file and add some text to it.
- Display the contents of an existing file.

```
# include <stdio.h>
int main( )
{
    char ch, str[ 10 ] ;
    while ( ( ch = getc ( stdin ) ) != -1 )
        putc ( ch, stdout ) ;
    return 0 ;
}
```

*Answer:*

Assuming that the above program is stored in a file 'Sample.c', on compilation a file 'Sample.exe' would get created.

To copy the contents of one file into another:

C:>Sample.exe < trial.txt > newtrial.txt

To create a new file and add some text to it:

C:>Sample.exe > trial.txt

To display the contents of an existing file:

C:>Sample.exe < trial.txt

(b) State True or False:

(1) We can send arguments at command-line even if we define **main( )** function without parameters.

Answer: False

(2) To use standard file pointers we don't need to open the file using **fopen( )**.

Answer: True

(3) The zeroth element of **argv** array always points to the name of the executable file.

Answer: False

(c) Write a program using command-line arguments to search for a word in a file and replace it with the specified word. The usage of the program is shown below.

C> change <old word> <new word> <filename>

*Program:*

```
# include <stdio.h>
# include <stdlib.h>
# include <string.h>
FILE *fs, *ft ;
int newstr ( char  *, char  *, char *  ) ;
int main ( int argc, char *argv[  ] )
{
    char  str[ 80 ] ;
    int newstr ( char  *s, char  *t, char *n ) ;
    if ( argc != 4 )
    {
        puts ( "Improper number of arguments\n" ) ;
        exit ( 1 ) ;
    }
```

```
    fs = fopen ( argv[ 3 ], "r" ) ;
    printf ( "%s \n %s \n %s \n %s", argv[0], argv[1],
            argv[2], argv[3]) ;
    if ( fs == NULL )
    {
        puts ( "Unable to open source file\n" ) ;
        exit ( 2 ) ;
    }
    ft = fopen ( "temp.txt", "w" ) ;
    if ( ft == NULL )
    {
        puts ( "Unable to open target file\n" ) ;
        fclose ( fs ) ;
        exit ( 3 ) ;
    }
    while ( fgets ( str, 79, fs ) != NULL )
        newstr ( str, argv[ 1 ], argv[ 2 ] ) ;
    fclose ( fs ) ;
    fclose ( ft ) ;
    remove ( argv[ 3 ] ) ;
    rename ( "temp.txt", argv[ 3 ] ) ;
    return 0 ;
}
int newstr ( char  *line, char  *search, char *replace  )
{
    char *p ;
    int offset ;
    char pre[ 80 ], post[ 80 ], final[ 80 ] ;
    p = strstr ( line, search ) ;
    if ( p == NULL )
        return ;
    offset = p - line ;
    strncpy ( pre, line, offset ) ;
    pre[ offset ] = '\0' ;
    strcpy ( post, p + strlen ( search ) ) ;
    strcpy ( final, pre ) ;
    strcat ( final, replace ) ;
    strcat ( final, post ) ;
    fputs ( final, ft ) ;
}
```

(d) Write a program that can be used at command prompt as a calculating utility. The usage of the program is shown below.

C> calc <switch> <n> <m>

where, **n** and **m** are two integer operands and **switch** is either an arithmetic operator or a comparison operator. If arithmetic operator is supplied, the output should be the result of the operation. If comparison operator is supplied then the output should be **True** or **False**.

*Program:*

```
/* To perform the given arithmetic operation on the two integers */
# include <stdio.h>
# include <stdlib.h>
# include <string.h>
int main ( int argc, char *argv[ ] )
{
    int i, first, second, result ;
    /* arithmetic and logical operators */
    char *str[ ] = { "+", "-", "*", "/", "%", "<", ">", "<=", ">=",
                    "==", "!=" } ;
    /* check if proper no of arguments are passed */
    if ( argc != 4 )
    {
        puts ( "Improper number of arguments\n" ) ;
        exit ( 1 ) ;
    }
    /* check if the entered operator is valid */
    for ( i = 0 ; i <= 10 ; i++ )
    {
        if ( strcmp ( argv[ 1 ], str[ i ] ) == 0 )
            break ;
    }
    if ( i == 11 )
    {
        printf ( "\nNot a valid operator\n" ) ;
        exit ( 2 ) ;
    }
    first = atoi ( argv[ 2 ] ) ;
    second = atoi ( argv[ 3 ] ) ;
    printf ( "\nResult of the operation is:\n" ) ;
```

```
switch ( i )
{
    case 0 :
        result = first + second ;
        printf ( "%d\n", result ) ;
        break ;
    case 1 :
        result = first - second ;
        printf ( "%d\n", result ) ;
        break ;
    case 2 :
        result = first * second ;
        printf ( "%d\n", result ) ;
        break ;
    case 3 :
        result = first / second ;
        printf ( "%d\n", result ) ;
        break ;
    case 4 :
        result = first % second ;
        printf ( "%d\n", result ) ;
        break ;
    case 5 :
        result = first < second ;
        result == 0 ? printf ( "False\n" ) : printf ( "True\n" ) ;
        break ;
    case 6 :
        result = first > second ;
        result == 0 ? printf ( "False\n" ) : printf ( "True\n" ) ;
        break ;
    case 7 :
        result = first <= second ;
        result == 0 ? printf ( "False\n" ) : printf ( "True\n" ) ;
        break ;
    case 8 :
        result = first >= second ;
        result == 0 ? printf ( "False\n" ) : printf ( "True\n" ) ;
        break ;
    case 9 :
        result = first == second ;
        result == 0 ? printf ( "False\n" ) : printf ( "True\n" ) ;
```

```
            break ;
        case 10 :
            result = first != second ;
            result == 0 ? printf ( "False\n" ) : printf ( "True\n" ) ;
            break ;

    }
    return 0 ;
}
```

# CHAPTER TWENTY ONE

# Operations On Bits

**[A]** Attempt the following questions:

(a) In an inter-college competition, various sports like cricket, basketball, football, hockey, lawn tennis, table tennis, carom and chess are played between different colleges. The information regarding the games won by a particular college is stored in bit numbers 0, 1, 2, 3, 4, 5, 6, 7 and 8 of an integer variable **game**. The college that wins in 5 or more than 5 games is awarded the Champion of Champions trophy. If a number representing the bit pattern mentioned above is entered through the keyboard, then write a program to find out whether the college won the Champion of the Champions trophy or not, along with the names of the games won by the college.

*Program:*

```
/* Determine the games won */
# include <stdio.h>
int main( )
{
    int game ;
    int cnt, count = 0 ;
    printf ( "\nEnter any number: " ) ;
    scanf ( "%d", &game ) ;
    /* count the no of games won */
    for ( cnt = 1 ; cnt <= 256 ; cnt *= 2 )
    {
        if ( ( game & cnt ) == cnt ) /* bits 0 to 7 */
            count++ ;
    }
```

```
    printf ( "Matches won by the college are: %d\n", count ) ;
    if ( count >= 5 )
    {
        printf ( "College won Champion of Champions trophy\n" ) ;
        printf ( "The games won by the college are:\n" ) ;
        if ( ( game & 1 ) == 1 ) /* bit 0 */
            printf ( "Cricket\n" ) ;
        if ( ( game & 2 ) == 2 ) /* bit 1 */
            printf ( "Basketball\n" ) ;
        if ( ( game & 4 ) == 4 ) /* bit 2 */
            printf ( "Football\n" ) ;
        if ( ( game & 8 ) == 8 ) /* bit 3 */
            printf ( "Hockey\n" ) ;
        if ( ( game & 16 ) == 16 ) /* bit 4 */
            printf ( "Lawn tennis\n" ) ;
        if ( ( game & 32 ) == 32 ) /* bit 5 */
            printf ( "Table tennis\n" ) ;
        if ( ( game & 64 ) == 64 ) /* bit 6 */
            printf ( "Carom\n" ) ;
        if ( ( game & 128 ) == 128 ) /* bit 7 */
            printf ( "Chess\n" ) ;
    }
    return 0 ;
}
```

(b) An animal could be a canine (dog, wolf, fox, etc.), a feline (cat, lynx, jaguar, etc.), a cetacean (whale, narwhal, etc.) or a marsupial (koala, wombat, etc.). The information whether a particular animal is canine, feline, cetacean, or marsupial is stored in bit number 0, 1, 2 and 3 respectively of an integer variable **type**. Bit number 4 of the variable **type** stores the information about whether the animal is Carnivore or Herbivore.

For the following animal, complete the program to determine whether the animal is an herbivore or a carnivore. Also determine whether the animal is a canine, feline, cetacean or a marsupial.

```
struct animal
{
    char name[ 30 ] ;
    int type ;
}
```

```
struct animal  a = { "OCELOT", 18 } ;
```

*Program:*

```
/* Determine the type of animal */
# include <stdio.h>
int main( )
{
    struct animal
    {
        char name[ 30 ] ;
        int type ;
    } ;
    static struct animal a = { "OCELOT", 18 } ;
    int ani ;
    printf ( "\nAnimal is:" ) ;
    ani = a.type ;
    if ( ( ani & 1 ) == 1 ) /* bit 0 */
        printf ( "Canine\n" ) ;
    if ( ( ani & 2 ) == 2 ) /* bit 1 */
        printf ( "Feline\n" ) ;
    if ( ( ani & 4 ) == 4 ) /* bit 2 */
        printf ( "Catacean\n" ) ;
    if ( ( ani & 8 ) == 8 ) /* bit 3 */
        printf ( "Marsupial\n" ) ;
    printf ( "Animal is also a " ) ;
    if ( ( ani & 16 ) == 16 ) /* bit 4 */
        printf ( "Carnivore\n" ) ;
    else
        printf ( "Herbivore\n" ) ;
    return 0 ;
}
```

(c) In order to save disk space, information about student is stored in an integer variable. Bit numbers 0 to 3 indicate whether the student is a I$^{st}$ year, II$^{nd}$ year, III$^{rd}$ year or IV$^{th}$ year student respectively. Bits 4 to 7 indicate whether the student's stream is Mechanical, Chemical, Electronics or CS. Rest of the bits store room number. Such data for 4 students is stored in the following array:

```
int data[  ] = {  273, 548, 786, 1096 } ;
```

Write a program that uses this data and displays the information about the student.

*Program:*

```
/* Determine the year, branch and room number */
# include <stdio.h>
#define _BV( x ) 1 << x
int main( )
{
    int i, num, roomnum ;
    unsigned short int data[ ] = { 273, 548, 786, 1096 } ;
    for ( i = 0 ; i < 4 ; i++ )
    {
        num = data[ i ] ;
        if ( ( num & _BV( 0 ) ) == _BV( 0 ) )
            printf ( "Year: First year\n" ) ;
        if ( ( num & _BV( 1 ) ) == _BV( 1 ) )
            printf ( "Year: Second year\n" ) ;
        if ( ( num & _BV( 2 ) ) == _BV( 2 ) )
            printf ( "Year: Third year\n" ) ;
        if ( ( num & _BV( 3 ) ) == _BV( 3 ) )
            printf ( "Year: Fourth year\n" ) ;
        if ( ( num & _BV( 4 ) ) == _BV( 4 ) )
            printf ( "Branch: Mechanical\n" ) ;
        if ( ( num & _BV( 5 ) ) == _BV( 5 ) )
            printf ( "Branch: Chemical\n" ) ;
        if ( ( num & _BV( 6 ) ) == _BV( 6 ) )
            printf ( "Branch: Electronics\n" ) ;
        if ( ( num & _BV( 7 ) ) == _BV( 7 ) )
            printf ( "Branch: CS\n" ) ;
        roomnum = num >> 8 ;
        printf ( "Room number: %d\n", roomnum ) ;
    }
    return 0 ;
}
```

(d) What will be the output of the following program?

```
# include <stdio.h>
int main( )
{
```

```
    int i = 32, j = 65, k, l, m, n, o, p ;
    k = i | 35 ;
    l = ~k ;
    m = i & j ;
    n = j ^ 32 ;
    o = j << 2 ;
    p = i >> 5 ;
    printf ( "k = %d l = %d m = %d\n", k, l, m ) ;
    printf ( "n = %d o = %d p = %d\n", n, o, p ) ;
    return 0 ;
}
```

*Output:*

```
k = 35 l = -36 m = 0
n = 97 o = 260 p = 1
```

**[B]** Answer the following questions:

(a) What is hexadecimal equivalent of each of the following binary numbers?

| | |
|---|---|
| 01011010 | 11000011 |
| 1010101001110101 | 1111000001011010 |

*Answer:*

5A
C3
AA75
F05A

(b) Rewrite the following expressions using bitwise compound assignment operators:

```
a = a | 3
a = a & 0x48
b = b ^ 0x22
c = c << 2
```

*Answer:*

```
a |= 3 ;
a &= 0x48 ;
```

```
b ^= 0x22 ;
c <<= 2 ;
```

(c) Consider an unsigned integer in which rightmost bit is numbered as 0. Write a function **checkbits ( x, p, n )** which returns true if all "n" bits starting from position "p" are turned on. For example, **checkbits ( x, 4, 3 )** will return true if bits 4, 3 and 2 are 1 in number x.

*Program:*

```
# include <stdio.h>
#include <math.h>
# define _BV(x) ( 1 << x )
void showbits ( unsigned int ) ;
int checkbits ( unsigned int, int, int ) ;
int main( )
{
    unsigned int x = 0xF0FF ;
    int n, p ;
    int flag ;
    printf ( "Value of x = " ) ;
    showbits ( x ) ;
    printf ( "\n" ) ;
    printf ( "Enter position and number of bits:\n" ) ;
    scanf ( "%d %d", &p, &n ) ;
    flag = checkbits ( x, p, n ) ;
    if ( flag == 1 )
        printf ( "%d bits from pos %d are turned on\n", n, p ) ;
    else
        printf ( "%d bits from pos %d are not turned on\n", n, p ) ;
    return 0 ;
}
void showbits ( unsigned int n )
{
    int i ;
    unsigned int j, k, andmask ;
    for ( i = 15 ; i >= 0 ; i-- )
    {
        j = i ;
        k = n & _BV( j ) ;
```

```
        k == 0 ? printf ( "0" ) : printf ( "1" ) ;
    }
}
int checkbits ( unsigned int x, int p, int n )
{
    int i ;
    for ( i = 0 ; i < n ; i++ )
    {
        if ( x & _BV( p ) != _BV( p ) )
            return 0 ;
        p-- ;
    }
    return 1 ;
}
```

(d) Write a program to scan an 8-bit number into a variable and check whether its 3rd, 6th and 7th bit is on.

*Program:*

```
/* Program to check if 3rd, 6th and 7th bit of a number is on */
# include <stdio.h>
# define _BV(x) ( 1 << x )
void showbits ( unsigned char ) ;
int main( )
{
    unsigned char a ;
    unsigned int num ;
    printf ( "\nEnter a number: " ) ;
    scanf ( "%hu", &num ) ;
    num = num & 0x00FF ;
    a = num ;
    showbits ( num ) ;
    printf ( "\n" ) ;
    if ( ( a & _BV( 3 ) ) == _BV( 3 ) )
        printf ( "Its third bit is on\n" ) ;
    else
        printf ( "Its third bit is off\n" ) ;
    if ( ( a & _BV( 6 ) ) == _BV( 6 ) )
        printf ( "Its sixth bit is on\n" ) ;
    else
```

```
        printf ( "Its sixth bit is off\n" ) ;
    if ( ( a & _BV( 7 ) ) == _BV( 7 ) )
        printf ( "Its seventh bit is on\n" ) ;
    else
        printf ( "Its seventh bit is off\n" ) ;
    return 0 ;
}
void showbits ( unsigned char n )
{
    int i ;
    unsigned char k, andmask ;
    for ( i = 7 ; i >= 0 ; i-- )
    {
        andmask = 1 << i ;
        k = n & andmask ;
        k == 0 ? printf ( "0" ) : printf ( "1" ) ;
    }
}
```

(e) Write a program to receive an unsigned 16-bit integer and then exchange the contents of its two bytes using bitwise operators.

*Program:*

```
/* Program to exchange the contents of numbers two bytes */
# include <stdio.h>
void showbits ( unsigned int ) ;
int main( )
{
    unsigned short int num, leftbyte, rightbyte, newnum ;
    printf ( "Enter a number: " ) ;
    scanf ( "%hu", &num ) ;
    showbits ( num ) ;
    printf ( "\n" ) ;
    leftbyte = ( num & 0xFF00 ) >> 8 ;
    rightbyte = num & 0x00FF ;
    newnum = ( rightbyte << 8 ) | leftbyte ;
    printf ( "New number after exchanging bytes: " ) ;
    showbits ( newnum ) ;
    printf ( "\n" ) ;
    return 0 ;
```

```
}
void showbits ( unsigned int n )
{
    int i ;
    unsigned int j, k, andmask ; for ( i = 15 ; i >= 0 ; i-- )
    {
        j = i ;
        andmask = 1 << j ;
        k = n & andmask ;
        k == 0 ? printf ( "0" ) : printf ( "1" ) ;
    }
}
```

(f) Write a program to receive an 8-bit number into a variable and then exchange its higher 4 bits with lower 4 bits.

*Program:*

```
/* Program to exchange the contents of numbers two bytes */
# include <stdio.h>
void showbits ( unsigned int ) ;
int main( )
{
    unsigned short int num ;
    unsigned char a, leftnibble, rightnibble, newnum ;
    printf ( "Enter a number: " ) ;
    scanf ( "%hu", &num ) ;
    a = num & 0x00FF ;
    showbits ( num ) ;
    printf ( "\n" ) ;
    leftnibble = ( a & 0xF0 ) >> 4 ;
    rightnibble = a & 0x0F ;
    newnum = ( rightnibble << 4 ) | leftnibble ;
    printf ( "New number after exchanging nibbles: " ) ;
    showbits ( newnum ) ;
    printf ( "\n" ) ;
    return 0 ;
}
void showbits ( unsigned char n )
{
    int i ;
```

```
    unsigned char j, k, andmask ;
    for ( i = 7 ; i >= 0 ; i-- )
    {
        j = i ;
        andmask = 1 << j ;
        k = n & andmask ;
        k == 0 ? printf ( "0" ) : printf ( "1" ) ;
    }
}
```

(g) Write a program to receive an 8-bit number into a variable and then set its odd bits to 1.

*Program:*

```
# include <stdio.h>
# define _BV(x) ( 1 << x )
void showbits ( unsigned char n ) ;
int main( )
{
    unsigned char a, b, c ;
    unsigned int num ;
    printf ( "Enter a number\n" ) ;
    scanf ( "%hu", &num ) ;
    num = num & 0x00FF ;
    a = num ;
    b = _BV(1) | _BV(3) | _BV(5) | _BV(7);
    a = a | b ; showbits ( a ) ;
    printf ( "\n" ) ;
}
void showbits ( unsigned char n )
{
    int i ;
    unsigned char j, k, andmask ;
    for ( i = 7 ; i >= 0 ; i-- )
    {
        j = i ;
        andmask = 1 << j ;
        k = n & andmask ;
        k == 0 ? printf ( "0" ) : printf ( "1" ) ;
    }
```

```
}
```

(h) Write a program to receive an 8-bit number into a variable and then check if its 3[rd] and 5[th] bit are on. If these bits are found to be on then put them off.

*Program:*

```
# include <stdio.h>
# define _BV(x) ( 1 << x )
void showbits ( unsigned char n ) ;
int main( )
{
    unsigned char a, mask ;
    short unsigned int num ;
    printf ( "Enter a number\n" ) ;
    scanf ( "%hu", &num ) ;
    num = num & 0x00FF ;
    a = num ;
    printf ( "a = " ) ;
    showbits ( a ) ;
    printf ( "\n" ) ;
    mask = _BV( 3 ) ;
    if ( ( a & mask ) == mask )
    {
        printf ( "3rd bit is on... will put it off\n" ) ;
        a = a & ~mask ;
        printf ( "a = " ) ;
        showbits ( a ) ;
        printf ( "\n" ) ;
    }
    else
        printf ( "3rd bit is on\n" ) ;
    mask = _BV( 5 ) ;
    if ( ( a & mask ) == mask )
    {
        printf ( "5th bit is on... will put it off\n" ) ;
        a = a & ~mask ;
        printf ( "a = " ) ;
        showbits ( a ) ;
        printf ( "\n" ) ;
```

```
        }
        else
            printf ( "5th bit is off\n" ) ;
    }
    void showbits ( unsigned char n )
    {
        int i ;
        unsigned char j, k, andmask ;
        for ( i = 7 ; i >= 0 ; i-- )
        {
            j = i ;
            andmask = 1 << j ; k = n & andmask ;
            k == 0 ? printf ( "0" ) : printf ( "1" ) ;
        }
    }
```

(i) Write a program to receive an 8-bit number into a variable and then check if its 3rd and 5th bit are off. If these bits are found to be off then put them on.

*Program:*

```
# include <stdio.h>
# define _BV(x) ( 1 << x )
void showbits ( unsigned char n ) ;
int main( )
{
    unsigned  char  a, mask ;
    short unsigned int num ;
    printf ( "Enter a number\n" ) ;
    scanf ( "%hu", &num ) ;
    num = num & 0x00FF ;
    a = num ;
    printf ( "a = " ) ;
    showbits ( a ) ;
    printf ( "\n" ) ;
    mask = _BV( 3 ) ;
    if ( ( a & mask ) == mask )
        printf ( "3rd bit is on\n" ) ;
    else
    {
```

```
            printf ( "3rd bit is off... will put it on\n" ) ;
            a = a | mask ;
            printf ( "a = " ) ;
            showbits ( a ) ;
            printf ( "\n" ) ;
        }
        mask = _BV( 5 ) ;
        if ( ( a & mask ) == mask )
            printf ( "5th bit is on\n" ) ;
        else
        {
            printf ( "5th bit is off... will put it on\n" ) ;
            a = a | mask ;
            printf ( "a = " ) ;
            showbits ( a ) ;
            printf ( "\n" ) ;
        }
    }
    void showbits ( unsigned char n )
    {
        int i ;
        unsigned char j, k, andmask ;
        for ( i = 7 ; i >= 0 ; i-- )
        {
            j = i ;
            andmask = 1 << j ;
            k = n & andmask ;
            k == 0 ? printf ( "0" ) : printf ( "1" ) ;
        }
    }
```

(j) Rewrite the **showbits( )** function used in this chapter using the **BV** macro.

*Program:*

```
# define _BV(x) ( 1 << x )
void showbits ( unsigned char n )
{
    int i ;
    unsigned char j, k ;
```

```
    for ( i = 7 ; i >= 0 ; i-- )
    {
        j = i ;
        k = n & _BV( j ) ;
        k == 0 ? printf ( "0" ) : printf ( "1" ) ;
    }
}
```

# CHAPTER TWENTY TWO

# Miscellaneous Features

**[A]** What will be the output of the following programs?

(a)
```
# include <stdio.h>
int main( )
{
    enum status { pass, fail, atkt } ;
    enum status  stud1, stud2, stud3 ;
    stud1 = pass ;
    stud2 = fail ;
    stud3 = atkt ;
    printf ( "%d %d %d\n", stud1, stud2, stud3 ) ;
    return 0 ;
}
```

*Output:*

0 1 2

(b)
```
# include <stdio.h>
int main( )
{
    printf ( "%f\n", ( float ) ( ( int ) 3.5 / 2 ) ) ;
    printf ( "%d\n", ( int ) ( ( ( float ) 3 / 2 ) * 3 ) ) ;
    return 0 ;
}
```

*Output:*

1.000000
4

**[B]** Point out the error, if any, in the following programs:

(a)
```
# include <stdio.h>
int main( )
{
    typedef struct patient
    {
        char name[ 20 ] ; int age ;
        int systolic_bp ; int diastolic_bp ;
    } ptt ;
    ptt p1 = { "anil", 23, 110, 220 } ;
    printf ( "%s %d\n", p1.name, p1.age ) ;
    printf ( "%d %d\n", p1.systolic_bp, p1.diastolic_bp ) ;
    return 0 ;
}
```

No Error

(b)
```
# include <stdio.h>
void show( ) ;
int main( )
{
    void ( *s )( ) ;
    s = show ;
    ( *s )( ) ;
    s( ) ;
    return 0 ;
}
void show( )
{
    printf ( "don't show off. It won't pay in the long run\n" ) ;
}
```

No Error

(c)
```
# include <stdio.h>
void show ( int, float ) ;
int main( )
{
    void ( *s )( int, float ) ;
    s = show ;
    ( *s )( 10, 3.14 ) ;
    return 0 ;
```

```
}
void show ( int  i, float  f )
{
    printf ( "%d %f\n", i, f ) ;
}
```

No Error

**[C]** Attempt the following questions:

(a) Write a program, which stores information about a date in a structure containing three members—day, month and year. Using bit fields, the day number should get stored in first 5 bits of day, the month number in 4 bits of month and year in 12 bits of year. Write a program to read date of joining of 10 employees and display them in ascending order of year.

*Program:*

```
/* To store joining dates using bit fields */
# include <stdio.h>
int main( )
{
    struct date
    {
        unsigned day : 5 ;
        unsigned month : 4 ;
        unsigned year : 12 ;
    } ;
    struct date dt[ 10 ], temp ;
    int i, j, d, m, y ;
    printf ( "Enter joining dates (dd-mm-yyyy) of 10 employees\n" ) ;
    for ( i = 0 ; i < 10 ; i++ )
    {
        scanf ( "%d %d %d", &d, &m, &y ) ;
        if ( d < 1 || d > 31 || m < 1 || m > 12 )
        {
            printf ( "Invalid date, enter new date\n" ) ;
            i-- ;
            continue ;
        }
        dt[ i ].day = d ;
```

```
        dt[ i ].month = m ;
        dt[ i ].year = y ;
    }
    for ( i = 0 ; i < 9 ; i++ )
    {
        for ( j = i + 1 ; j < 10 ; j++ )
        {
            if ( dt[ j ].year < dt[ i ].year )
            {
                temp = dt[ i ] ;
                dt[ i ] = dt[ j ] ;
                dt[ j ] = temp ;
            }
        }
    }
    for ( i = 0 ; i < 10 ; i++ )
        printf ( "%d %d %d\n", dt[ i ].day, dt[ i ].month, dt[ i ].year ) ;
    return 0 ;
}
```

(b) Write a program to read and store information about insurance policy holder. The information contains details like gender, whether the holder is minor/major, policy name and duration of the policy. Make use of bit-fields to store this information.

*Program:*

```
/* To store information about insurance policy holder */
#include <stdio.h>
# include <string.h>
int main( )
{
    struct policy_holder
    {
        unsigned gender : 1 ;   // 0-Male, 1-Female
        unsigned status : 1 ;   // 0-Minor, 1-Major
        char name[ 20 ] ;
        unsigned dr : 5 ;
    } ;
    struct policy_holder h ;
    int g, s, d ;
    char n[ 20 ] ;
```

```
    printf ( "\nEnter gender (0-Male, 1-Female): " ) ;
    scanf ( "%d", &g ) ;
    printf ( "\nEnter status (0-Minor, 1-Major): " ) ;
    scanf ( "%d", &s ) ;
    printf ( "\nEnter name of the policy holder: " ) ;
    scanf ( "%s", n ) ;
    printf ( "\nEnter duration (1 to 25 yrs) of the policy: " ) ;
    scanf ( "%d", &d ) ;
    h.gender = g ;
    h.status = s ;
    strcpy ( h.name, n ) ;
    h.dr = d ;
    printf ( "Name: %s\n", h.name ) ;
    printf ( "Gender: %s\n", h.gender == 0 ? "Male" : "Female" ) ;
    printf ( "Status: %s\n", h.status == 0 ? "Minor" : "Major" ) ;
    printf ( "Duration %d\n", h.dr ) ;
    return 0 ;
}
```

CHAPTER

# TWENTY THREE

# Periodic Tests
# Course Tests

## Periodic Test I

**[A]** Fill in the blanks: [5 Marks, 1 Mark each]

(1) The expression **i++** is same as ++i .

(2) Real / float / double type of values cannot be checked using **switch-case**.

(3) Every instruction in a C program must end with a ;.

(4) The size of an **int** data type is 4 bytes.

(5) Statements written in do-while loop get executed at least once even if the condition is false.

**[B]** State True or False: [5 Marks, 1 Mark each]

(1) The statement **for ( ; ; )** is a valid statement. **True**

(2) The **else** clause in an **if – else if – else** statement goes to work if all the **if**s fail. **True**

(3) The ^ operator is used for performing exponentiation operations in C. **False**

(4) C allows only one variable on the left-hand side of = operator. **True**

(5) Conditional operators cannot be nested. **False**

**[C]** What would be the output of the following programs?
[5 Marks, 1 Mark each]

5 5 6
65 A
2 1
21 525
0 1

**[D]** Point out the error, if any, in the following programs:
[5 Marks, 1 Mark each]

Use == instead of =
'then' : undeclared identifier
Syntax error: missing ' ; ' before ':'.
No Error.
No Error.

**[E]** Attempt the following questions: [20 Marks, 5 Marks each]

(1) Write a program to calculate the sum of the following series:

1! 2! + 2! 3! + 3! 4! + 4! 5! + ...... + 9! 10!

```
#include <stdio.h>
int main( )
{
    int i, j ;
    float prod1, prod2, term, s ;
    s = 0 ;
    for ( i = 1 ; i <= 10 ; i++ )
    {
        prod1 = 1 ;
        for ( j = 1 ; j <= i ; j++ )
            prod1 = prod1 * j ;
        prod2 = prod1 * j ;
        term = prod1 * prod2 ;
        s = s + term ;
    }
    printf ( "sum of series = %f\n", s ) ;
    return 0 ;
}
```

(2) Write a program to enter the numbers till the user wants and at the end it should display the count of positive, negative and zeros entered.

```
#include <stdio.h>
int main( )
{
```

```
    int  neg, pos, zero, n ;
    char ch = 'y' ;
    pos = neg = zero = 0 ;
    while ( ch == 'y' || ch == 'Y' )
    {
        printf ( "Enter a number: \n" ) ;
        scanf ( "%d", &n ) ;
        if ( n > 0 )
            pos++ ;
        if ( n < 0 )
            neg++ ;
        if ( n == 0 )
            zero++ ;
        printf ( "Do you want to continue y/n" ) ;
        fflush ( stdin ) ;
        scanf ( "%c", &ch ) ;
    }
    printf ( "Positive = %d\n", pos ) ;
    printf ( "Negative = %d\n", neg ) ;
    printf ( "Zeros = %d\n", zero ) ;
    return 0 ;
}
```

(3) Write a program to find the range of a set of numbers that are input through the keyboard. Range is the difference between the smallest and biggest number in the list.

```
#include<stdio.h>
int main( )
{
    int  n, no, flag, small, big ;
    flag = 0 ;
    printf ( "Enter the number of elements in the range:\n" ) ;
    scanf ( "%d", &n ) ;
    while ( n > 0 )
    {
        printf ( "Enter a number:\n" ) ;
        scanf ( "%d", &no ) ;
        if ( flag == 0 )
        {
            small = big = no ;
```

```
                flag = 1 ;
            }
            else
            {
                if ( no > big )
                    big = no ;
                if ( no < small )
                    small = no ;
            }
            n-- ;
        }
        printf ( "Range: %d", big - small ) ;
        return 0 ;
    }
```

(4) If three integers are entered through the keyboard, write a program to determine whether they form a Pythagorean triplet or not.

```
#include<stdio.h>
int main( )
{
    int i, j, k ;
    printf ( "Enter three integers: \n" ) ;
    scanf ( "%d%d%d", &i, &j, &k ) ;
    if ( ( i * i + j * j == k * k ) || ( j * j + k * k == i * i ) ||
        ( k * k + i * i == j * j ) )
        printf ( "Numbers form pythogorean triplet \n" ) ;
    else
        printf ( "Numbers do not form pythogorean triplet \n" ) ;
    return 0 ;
}
```

## Periodic Test II

**[A]** Fill in the blanks: [5 Marks, 1 Mark each]

(1) & and * are pointer operators.

(2) Pointers are variables, which hold addresses of other variables.

(3) & is called an 'address of' operator.

(4) The preprocessor directive that is used to give convenient names to difficult formulae is called macro expansion.

(5) For a call by reference, you should pass addresses of variables to the called function.

**[B]** State True or False: [5 Marks, 1 Mark each]

(1) A function can return more than one value at a time. **False**

(2) A fresh set of variables are created every time a function gets called. **True**

(3) All types of pointers are 4 bytes long. **True**

(4) Any function can be made a recursive function. **False**

(5) The correct build order is Preprocessing – Compilation – Assembling – Linking. **True**

**[C]** Answer the following questions: [10 Marks, 2 Marks each]

(1) Why are addresses of functions stored in the stack?

So that it would be possible to return to the same place from where the function was called, once the called function's execution is over.

(2) How do you decide whether a variable should be passed by value or by reference?

If we want that the passed variable's value should not change in the function being called use a call by value.

If we want that the passed variable's value should change in the function being called use a call by reference.

(3) Size of a pointer is not dependent on whose address is stored in it. Justify.

A pointer contains address. Any address is 4 byte long. So, it does not matter, whose address is held in a pointer, the pointer remains 4 bytes long.

(4) What different types of integer variables can be created in C? Which format specifier is used with each type in **printf( )**?

signed short int - %hd
unsigned short int - %hu
signed int - %d
unsigned - %u
signed long int - %ld
unsigned long int - %lu
signed long long int - %lld
unsigned long long int - %llu

(5) A recursive call should always be subjected to an **if**. Why? Explain with an example.

If the recursive call is not subjected to an **if**, the function would fall in an infinite loop.

```
void fun( )
{
    static int count = 0 ;
    count++ ;
    if ( count <= 5 )
    {
        printf ( "%d\n", count ) ;
        fun( ) ;
    }
    else
```

```
        return ;
}
```

**[D]** Attempt the following questions: [20 Marks, 5 Marks each]

(1) Define a function that receives 4 integers and returns sum, product and average of these integers.

```
#include <stdio.h>
void calc ( int *, int *, float * ) ;
int main( )
{
    int sum, prod ;
    float avg ;
    calc ( &sum, &prod, &avg ) ;
    printf ( "%d %d %f\n", sum, prod, avg ) ;
    return 0 ;
}
void calc ( int *sum, int *prod, float *avg )
{
    int n1, n2, n3, n4 ;
    printf ( "\n Enter four numbers :" ) ;
    scanf ( "%d%d%d%d", &n1, &n2, &n3, &n4 ) ;
    *sum = n1 + n2 + n3 + n4 ;
    *prod = n1 * n2 * n3 * n4 ;
    *avg = *sum / 4.0f ;
}
```

(2) Define a recursive function which prints the prime factors of the number that it receives when called from **main( )**.

```
#include <stdio.h>
void factor ( int ) ;
int main( )
{
    int num ;
    printf ( "\nEnter a number: " ) ;
    scanf ( "%d", &num ) ;
    printf ( "\nPrime Factors are: " ) ;
    factor ( num ) ;
    return 0 ;
```

```
}
void factor ( int n )
{
    static int i = 2 ;
    if ( i <= n )
    {
        if ( n % i == 0 )
        {
            printf ( "%d ", i ) ;
            n = n / i ;
        }
        else
            i++ ;
        factor ( n ) ;
    }
    return ;
}
```

(3) Define macros for calculating area of circle, circumference of circle, volume of a cone and volume of sphere.

```
#include <stdio.h>
#define PI  3.14f
#define ACI( r ) ( PI * r * r )
#define CCI( r ) ( 2 * PI * r )
#define VCO( r ) ( ( 1.0f / 3 ) * PI * r * r * r )
#define VCYL( r ) ( ( 4.0f / 3 ) * PI * r * r * r )
int main( )
{
    float  r, a_ci, c_ci, v_co, v_cyl ;
    printf ( "\n Enter the value of r :\n" ) ;
    scanf ( "%f", &r ) ;
    a_ci = ACI ( r ) ;
    c_ci = CCI ( r ) ;
    printf ( "\nArea of circle : %f", a_ci ) ;
    printf ( "\nCircumference of circle : %f", c_ci ) ;
    v_co = VCO ( r ) ;
    v_cyl = VCYL ( r ) ;
    printf ( "\n Volume of cone : %f",v_co ) ;
    printf ( "\n Volume of cylinder : %f", v_cyl ) ;
    return 0 ;
```

```
}
```

(4) Write a program that prints sizes of all types of chars, ints and reals.

```
#include <stdio.h>
int main( )
{
    char ch ;
    unsigned char dh ;
    printf ( "character = %d\n", sizeof ( ch ) ) ;
    printf ( "unsigned character = %d\n", sizeof ( dh ) ) ;
    short int a ;
    short unsigned int b ;
    int c ;
    long int d ;
    long unsigned int e ;
    printf ( "short signed integer = %d\n", sizeof ( a ) ) ;
    printf ( "short unsigned integer = %d\n", sizeof ( b ) ) ;
    printf ( "integer = %d\n", sizeof ( c ) ) ;
    printf ( "long signed integer = %d\n", sizeof ( d ) ) ;
    printf ( "long unsigned integer = %d\n", sizeof ( e ) ) ;
    float f ;
    double g ;
    long double h ;
    printf ( "float = %d\n", sizeof ( f ) ) ;
    printf ( "double = %d\n", sizeof ( g ) ) ;
    printf ( "long double = %d\n", sizeof ( h ) ) ;
    return 0 ;
}
```

## Periodic Test III

**[A]** Fill in the blanks: [5 Marks, 1 Mark each]

(1) Mentioning name of an array yields base address of the array.

(2) C permits us to exceed lower and upper bounds of an array.

(3) Size of an array is sum of sizes of individual elements of an array.

(4) Array elements are always counted from zero onwards.

(5) A structure is usually a collection of dissimilar elements.

**[B]** State True or False: [5 Marks, 1 Mark each]

(1) If an array's size is big its elements may get stored in non-adjacent locations. **False**

(2) All strings end with a '\0'. **True**

(3) Using **#pragma pack** you can control the layout of structure elements in memory. **True**

(4) Elements of 2-D array are stored in the form of rows and columns in memory. **False**

(5) 3-D array is a collection of several 1-D arrays. **False**

**[C]** Answer the following questions: [10 Marks, 2 Marks each]

(1) What is likely to happen if the bounds of an array are exceeded?

If bounds of an array are exceeded while reading, nothing will go wrong. However, if bounds are exceeded while writing to an array, something important that is already present beyond the bounds would get overwritten. Sometimes this may even hang the program. If the bounds of array are exceeded the compiler does not report an error "Subscript out of range". Bounds checking is always programmer's responsibility

(2) When you prefer a structure over an array to store similar elements? Explain with an example.

A structure is preferred over an array when a set of similar elements are to be returned from a function, because on attempting to return an array only its base address would get returned.

For example, if we are to return a complex number containing a real part and imaginary part (both floats) it is more convenient to put them into a structure rather than in an array.

(3) What is the limitation of an array of pointers to strings? How can it be overcome?

An array of pointers to strings is not very convenient if we are to receive strings into this array by reading them from keyboard. It can be overcome by first allocating space for strings using **malloc ( )** and then storing the addresses of strings into the array of pointers.

(4) In a two-dimensional array **a[ 4 ][ 4 ]**, why do expressions **a** and ***a** yield same base address?

**a** is supposed to give base address because **a**, the name of the array, acts as a pointer to the $0^{th}$ element of the array. A 2-D array is a collection of several 1-D arrays. So, when we use ***a**, we are referring to the $0^{th}$ 1-D array. And referring to 1-D array always yields its base address, hence ***a** also gives the base address.

(5) How will you allocate space for a **float** array whose size is received from the keyboard?

```
/* Method I */
# include <stdlib.h>
# include <stdio.h>
int main( )
{
    int sz ;
    float *fptr ;
    printf ( "Enter size of the array: " ) ;
    scanf ( "%d", &sz ) ;
```

```
    fptr = ( float * ) malloc ( sz * sizeof ( float ) ) ;
}

/* Method II */
# include <stdio.h>
int main( )
{
    int sz ;
    printf ( "Enter size of the array: " ) ;
    scanf ( "%d", &sz ) ;
    float arr[ sz ] ;
}
```

**[D]** Attempt the following questions: [20 Marks, 5 Marks each]

(1) Write a function that receives as parameters, a 1-D array, its size and an integer and returns number of times the integer occurs in the array.

```
#include <stdio.h>
int countnum ( int*, int, int ) ;
int main( )
{
    int arr[ 100 ], size, num, i, count ;
    printf ( "Enter the size of array:\n" ) ;
    scanf ( "%d", &size ) ;
    printf ( "Enter the elements of an array:\n" ) ;
    for ( i = 0 ; i < size ; i++ )
        scanf ( "%d", &arr[ i ] ) ;
    printf ( "Enter the number you want to count:\n" ) ;
    scanf ( "%d", &num ) ;
    count = countnum ( arr, size, num ) ;
    printf ( "count = %d", count ) ;
    return 0 ;
}
int countnum ( int *a, int sz, int n )
{
    int j, cnt = 0 ;
    for ( j = 0 ; j < sz ; j++ )
    {
        if ( *a == n )
            cnt++ ;
```

```
        a++ ;
    }
    return cnt ;
}
```

(2) Create an array of pointers containing names of 10 cities. Write a program that sorts the cities in reverse alphabetical order and prints this reversed list.

```
#include <stdio.h>
#include <string.h>
int main( )
{
    char *cities[ ] = {
                        "Nagpur", "Kanpur", "Delhi",
                        "Sikandarabad", "Akola", "Ghatanji",
                        "Jabalpur", "Ziri", "Shegaon", "Bombay"
                    } ;
    char  *t ;
    int  i, j ;
    for ( i = 0 ; i < 9 ; i++ )
    {
        for ( j = i + 1 ; j < 10 ; j++ )
        {
            if ( strcmp ( cities[ i ], cities[ j ] ) < 0 )
            {
                t = cities[ i ] ;
                cities[ i ] = cities[ j ] ;
                cities[ j ] = t ;
            }
        }
    }
    for ( i = 0 ; i < 10 ; i++ )
        printf ( "%s\n", cities[ i ] ) ;
    return 0 ;
}
```

(3) Declare a structure called **student** containing his name, age and address. Create and initialize three structure variables. Define a function to which these variables are passed. The function should

convert the names into uppercase. Print the resultant structure variables.

```
#include <stdio.h>
#include <string.h>
void upper ( struct stud* ) ;
struct stud
{
    char name[ 20 ] ;
    int age ;
    char addr[ 40 ] ;
} ;
struct stud s1 = { "akshay", 20, "Ravinagar" } ;
struct stud s2 = { "shubham", 21, "Civil Lines" } ;
struct stud s3 = { "nilesh", 22, "Khamla" } ;
int main( )
{
    upper ( &s1 ) ;
    upper ( &s2 ) ;
    upper ( &s3 ) ;
    return 0 ;

}
void upper ( struct stud *s )
{
    printf ( "Before conversion:\n" ) ;
    printf ( "%s %d %s\n", s->name, s->age, s->addr ) ;
    strupr ( s->name ) ;
    printf ( "After conversion:\n" ) ;
    printf ( "%s %d %s\n", s->name, s->age, s->addr ) ;
}
```

(4) Write a program that checks and reports whether sum of elements in the $i^{th}$ row of a 5 x 5 array is equal to sum of elements in $i^{th}$ column.

```
#include <stdio.h>
int main( )
{
    int a[ 5 ][ 5 ], i, j, sumr = 0, sumc = 0 ;
    printf ( "Enter elements of a 5 x 5 array\n" ) ;
```

```
    for ( i = 0 ; i < 5 ; i++ )
        for ( j = 0 ; j < 5 ; j++ )
            scanf ( "%d", &a[ i ][ j ] ) ;
    printf ( "Enter row and column you wish to check\n" ) ;
    scanf ( "%d", &i ) ;
    for ( j = 0 ; j < 5 ; j++ )
        sumr = sumr + a[ i - 1 ][ j ] ;
    for ( j = 0 ; j < 5 ; j++ )
        sumc = sumc + a[ j ][ i - 1 ] ;
    if ( sumr == sumc )
        printf ( "Sums are equal" ) ;
    else
        printf ( "Sums are not equal" ) ;
    return 0 ;
}
```

## Periodic Test IV

**[A]** Fill in the blanks: [5 Marks, 1 Mark each]

(1) 0xAABB | 0xBBAA evaluates to 0xBBBB.

(2) The values of an **enum** are stored as integers.

(3) An existing data type can be given a new name using the typedef keyword.

(4) The >> operator can be used to eliminate 3 least significant bits from a character.

(5) The ~ operator is used to invert the bits in a byte.

**[B]** State True or False: [5 Marks, 1 Mark each]

(1) To check whether a particular bit in a byte is on or off, the bitwise | operator is useful. **False**

(2) It is possible to create a union of structures. **True**

(3) The callback mechanism can be implemented using function pointers. **True**

(4) On evaluating the expression **a ^ 5** value of **a** would change. **False**

(5) Bitwise operators can work on **float**s and **double**s. **False**

**[C]** Answer the following questions: [10 Marks, 2 Marks each]

(1) What is the utility of <<, >>, & and | bitwise operators?

**<<, >>** operators are useful to shift out bits in a number from left or right. **&** is used to check whether a bit is on or off, and to set a particular bit to 0. **|** operator is used to put on a bit.

(2) Define the **_BV** macro. How would the following expressions involving the **_BV** macro be expanded by the preprocessor?

```
int a = _BV ( 5 ) ;
int b = ~ _BV ( 5 ) ;

#define _BV( x ) 1 << x
int a = _BV(5)   is expanded to  int a = 1 << 5
int b = ~ _BV(5) is expanded to  int b = ~ ( 1 << 5 )
```

(3) In the following expression what does **p** signify?

```
long ( *p[ 3 ] ) ( int, float ) ;
```

In this declaration **p** is an array of three function pointers, each pointer points to a function that receives an **int** and a **float** and returns a **long int**.

(4) Suggest a suitable **printf( )** that can be used to print the grocery items and their prices in the following format:

```
Tomato Sauce        : Rs. 225.50
Liril Soap          : Rs.  55.45
Pen Refill          : Rs.   8.95
```

```
printf ( "\n%25s:Rs. %8.2f\n", item, price ) ;
```

(5) When it is useful to make use of a union? What is the size of a union variable? How can the elements of a union variable be accessed?

We should use a union when we wish to access same memory locations in multiple ways. Size of a union variable is size of the biggest element in the union. Elements of a union variable can be accessed using the . and -> operators.

**[D]** Attempt the following questions: [20 Marks, 5 Marks each]

(1) Write a program to multiply two integers using bitwise operators.

```
#include <stdio.h>
int add ( int, int ) ;
int main( )
{
    int a, b, result ;
```

```
    printf ( "\nEnter the numbers to be multiplied :" ) ;
    scanf ( "%d%d", &a, &b ) ;
    result = 0 ;
    while ( b != 0 )
    {
        if (b & 1 )
            result = add ( result, a ) ;
        a <<= 1 ;
        b >>= 1 ;
    }
    printf ( "Result:%d", result ) ;
}
int add ( int x, int y )
{
    while ( y != 0 )
    {
        int carry = x & y ;
        x = x ^ y ;
        y = carry << 1 ;
    }
    return x ;
}
```

(2) Write a program to count number of words in a given text file.

```
#include <stdio.h>
#include <stdlib.h>
int main( )
{
    char ch ; FILE *fp ;
    char fname[ 67 ] ;
    int count = 0 ;
    printf ( "Enter File name: " ) ;
    gets ( fname ) ;
    fp = fopen ( fname, "r" ) ;
    if ( fp == NULL )
    {
        printf ("Unable to open file\n" ) ;
        exit ( 1 ) ;
    }
    while ( ( ch = getc ( fp ) ) != EOF )
```

```
    {
        if ( ch == ' ' )
            count++ ;
    }
    printf ( "No of words = %d", count + 1 ) ;
    fclose ( fp ) ;
}
```

(3) Write a program that receives a set of numbers as command- line arguments and prints their average.

```
#include <stdio.h>
#include <stdlib.h>
int main ( int  argc, char*  argv[ ] )
{
    int  sum, i, avg ;
    sum = 0 ;
    for ( i = 1 ; i < argc ; i++ )
        sum = sum + atoi ( argv[ i ] ) ;
    avg = sum / ( argc - 1 ) ;
    printf ( "Average = %d", avg ) ;
    return 0 ;
}
```

(4) Write a program to check whether contents of the two files are same by comparing them on a byte-by-byte basis.

```
#include <stdio.h>
#include <stdlib.h>
int  main( )
{
    char  ch1,ch2 ;
    FILE  *fp,*fq ;
    char  fname1[ 67 ], fname2[ 67 ] ;
    printf ( "Enter File1 name: " ) ;
    gets ( fname1 ) ;
    printf ( "Enter File2 name: " ) ;
    gets ( fname2 ) ;
    fp = fopen ( fname1, "rb" ) ;
    if ( fp == NULL )
    {
```

```
        printf ("Unable to open file1\n" ) ;
        exit ( 1 ) ;
    }
    fq = fopen ( fname2, "rb" ) ;
    if ( fq == NULL )
    {
        printf ("Unable to open file2\n" ) ;
        exit ( 1 ) ;
    }
    while ( 1 )
    {
        ch1 = getc ( fp ) ;
        ch2 = getc ( fq ) ;
        if ( ch1 == EOF && ch2 == EOF )
        {
            printf ( "File contents match" ) ;
            break ;
        }

        if ( ch1 != ch2  ||  ch1 == EOF && ch2 != EOF  ||
            ch1 != EOF && ch2 == EOF )
        {
            printf ( "File contents do not match" ) ;
            break ;
        }
    }
    fclose ( fp ) ;
    fclose ( fq ) ;
}
```

## Course Test I

**[A]** Fill in the blanks: [5 Marks, 1 Mark each]

(1) A function that calls itself is known as a recursive function.

(2) Preprocessor directives always begin with #.

(3) The expression **a[ i ][ j ]** in pointer notation is * ( * ( a + i ) + j ).

(4) A string always ends with the character '\0'.

(5) The keywords used to implement a case control instruction are switch, case and default.

**[B]** State True or False: [5 Marks, 1 Mark each]

| | |
|---|---|
| Shifts bits to left | << |
| Convert a bit to 0 | & |
| Compound assignment operator | *= |
| Put on a bit | \| |
| Typecast operator | a = ( int ) b |
| Toggle bits | ^ |
| Pre-increment operator | ++j |
| Comparison operator | == |
| Modulus operator | % |
| Conditional operators | ? : |

**[C]** Answer the following questions: [5 Marks, 1 Mark each]

(1) Dynamically allocate space for a 3-D array of dimensions 3 x 5 x 4. Set up each elements of this array with a value 10. Report an error, if enough memory space is not available.

```
#include <stdio.h>
#include <stdlib.h>
int main( )
{
    int i, j, k ;
    int *a ;
```

```
    a = ( int * ) malloc ( 3 * 5 * 4 * sizeof ( int ) ) ;
    if ( a == NULL )
        printf ( "Insufficient space\n" ) ;
    for ( i = 0 ; i < 3 ; i++ )
    {
        for ( j = 0 ; j < 5 ; j++ )
        {
            for ( k = 0 ; k < 4 ; k++ )
            {
                *( a + i * 5 * 4 + j * 4 + k ) = 10 ;
                printf ( "%d ", *( a + i * 5 * 4 + j * 4 + k ) = 10 ) ;
            }
            printf ( "\n" ) ;
        }
        printf ( "\n\n" ) ;
    }
}
```

(2) Create an array of pointers to strings for storing names of 5 persons. What is the limitation of this array?

```
int *names[ 5 ] ;
```

When we are using an array of pointers to strings, we can initialize the strings at the place where are declaring the array, but we cannot receive the strings from keyboard using **scanf( )**.

(3) Create a data structure for storing following data:

Name of the fruit
Color of the fruit
Diameter of the fruit
Price of the fruit
Weight of the fruit

```
struct fruit
{
   char name, color ;
   float dia, price, weight ;
} ;
struct fruit f1, f2, f3, f4, f5 ;
```

(4) If a function is to be called, is it necessary to mention its prototype declaration? If yes, why?

Yes, it is necessary to mention the prototype declaration of a function before calling it. This is because, during compilation it is checked whether the name, arguments and return type of the function being called matches with the prototype declaration.

(5) For a file being pointed to by **FILE *fp**, write function calls for carrying out the following operations?

- Set pointer at 5th position from beginning of file.
- Set pointer at 20th position from current position.
- Set pointer at 15th position before end of file.

```
fseek ( p, 5L, SEEK_SET ) ;
fseek ( p, 20L, SEEK_CUR ) ;
fseek ( p, -15L, SEEK_END ) ;
```

(6) Suppose there is a user-defined file called 'myfunctions.h'.

- Write a statement to include this file in you program?
- What provision will you make in 'myfunctions.h' to prevent it from getting included twice?

```
# include "myfunctions.h"
```

Following provision should be made in 'myfunctions.h' to prevent it from getting included twice:

```
/* myfunctions.h */
# ifndef __myfunctions_h
   # define __myfunctions_h
   /* some declarations */
# endif
```

(7) What do **argc** and **argv** represent with regards to command-line arguments?

**argc** contains number of arguments passed to the program while executing it at command-line.

**argv** is an array of pointers to strings. These pointers point to strings supplied at command-line. Thus address of the $n^{th}$ string is stored in **agrv[ n ]**.

(8) How will you redefine the types **unsigned long int** to **ULI** and **int **** to **DOUBLEPTR**? What is the scope of a **typedef** statement?

```
typedef unsigned long int ULI ;
typedef int** DOUBLEPTR ;
```

Scope of **typedef** is local if it is declared inside a function. The scope is global if it is declared outside all functions.

(9) Point out errors, in any, in the following code snippet:

```
int a ;
float b ;
char ch ;
scanf ( "%d %f %c", a, b, ch ) ;
printf ( "%d %f %c", &a, &b, &ch ) ;
```

Error. "&" should be used before each variable in **scanf( )**.

(10) What will be the output of the following code snippet?

```
int a = 10 , b = 20 , c= 0 ;
if ( a && b || c )
     printf ("Hello" ) ;
else
     printf( "Hi" ) ;

if ( !a && !b )
   printf ( "Good Morning!!" ) ;
else
     printf( "Good Evening" ) ;
```

```
Hello
Good Evening
```

**[D]** Attempt the following questions: [20 Marks, 5 Marks each]

(1) Write a program that defines a function called **isalnum( )**. The function should receive a string and check if all characters in it are alphabets or digits. If so, it should return a true, otherwise false. Call this function for the following strings:

"ABCD1234"
"Nagpur – 440010"

```
#include <stdio.h>
#define TRUE 1
#define FALSE 0
int isalnum ( char * ) ;
int main( )
{
    char str1[ ] = "ABCD1234" ;
    char str2[ ] = "Nagpur – 440010" ;
    int ret ;
    ret = isalnum ( str1 ) ;
    printf ( "%d\n", ret ) ;
    ret = isalnum ( str2 ) ;
    printf ( "%d\n", ret ) ;
}
int isalnum ( char *p )
{
    while ( *p )
    {
        if ( *p >= '0' && *p <= '9' || *p >= 'a' && *p <= 'z' ||
            *p >= 'A' && *p <= 'Z' )
            p++ ;
        else
            return FALSE ;
    }
    return TRUE ;
}
```

(2) Define an enumeration to represent colors red, green, yellow, magenta and brown. Create two variables **Apple** and **Banana** of this **enum** type and assign colors red and yellow to them respectively. Print these color values and indicate what output will they produce.

```
#include <stdio.h>
#include <stdlib.h>
int main( )
{
    enum fruits { red, green, yellow, magenta, brown } ;
    enum fruits Apple, Banana ;
    Apple = red ;
    Banana = yellow ;
    printf ( "%d %d\n", Apple, Banana ) ;
    return 0;
}
```

Output

0 2

(3) Define a function called **showbits( )** which displays all the bits of an **unsigned char** that it receives. Call this function for values 45 and 30. Indicate what output will **showbits( )** produce for these values?

```
# include <stdio.h>
void showbits ( unsigned char ) ;
int main( )
{
    unsigned char num1 = 45, num2 = 30 ;
    showbits ( num1 ) ;
    showbits ( num2 ) ;
    return 0 ;
}
void showbits ( unsigned char  n )
{
    int i ;
    unsigned char  j, k, andmask ;
    for ( i = 7 ; i >= 0 ; i-- )
    {
        j = i ;
        andmask = 1 << j ;
        k = n & andmask ;
        k == 0 ? printf ( "0" ) : printf ( "1" ) ;
    }
    printf ( "\n" ) ;
```

```
}
```

(4) Write a program to generate and print all unique combinations of numbers 1, 2, 3 and 4.

```
#include <stdio.h>
int main( )
{
   int i, j, k, l ;
   for ( i = 1 ; i <= 4 ; i++ )
   {
        for ( j = 1 ; j <= 4 ; j++ )
        {
             for ( k = 1 ; k <= 4 ; k++ )
             {
                  for ( l = 1 ; l <= 4 ; l++ )
                  {
                       if ( i != j && i != k && i != l && j != k && j != l
                            && k != l )
                            printf ( "%d %d %d %d\n", i, j, k, l ) ;
                  }
             }
        }
   }
   return 0 ;
}
```

(5) Define an iterative function and a recursive function to print first ten terms of a Fibonacci series. Which of these two functions will run faster and why?

```
/*Iterative Function*/
# include <stdio.h>
void ifibo ( int, int, int ) ;
void rfibo ( int, int, int, int ) ;
int main( )
{
   int first = 0, second = 1 ;
   printf ( "First 10 terms of Fibonacci series are:\n" ) ;
   ifibo ( first, second, 10 ) ;
   printf ( "\n" ) ;
```

```
    rfibo ( first, second, 0, 10 ) ;
    return 0 ;
}
void ifibo ( int old, int current, int terms )
{
    int newterm, i ;
    for ( i = 0 ; i < terms ; i++ )
    {
        if ( i <= 1 )
            newterm = i ;
        else
        {
            newterm = old + current ;
            old = current ;
            current = newterm ;
        }
        printf( "%d\t", newterm ) ;
    }
}
void rfibo ( int old, int current, int count, int terms )
{
    int  newterm ;
    if ( count == 0 || count == 1 )
    {
        printf ( "%d\t", count ) ;
        count++ ;
        terms-- ;
        rfibo ( old, current, count, terms ) ;
    }
    else if ( terms >= 1 )
    {
        newterm = old + current ;
        printf ( "%d\t", newterm ) ;
        terms = terms - 1 ;
        old = current ;
        current = newterm ;
        rfibo ( old, current, count, terms ) ;
    }
}
```

The iteration method would run faster as it involves only one function call.

## Course Test II

**[A]** State True or False: [5 Marks, 1 Mark each]

(1) Any function can be made a recursive function. False

(2) Macro expansion directive can be used to replace a complicated formula with a convenient template. True

(3) In the expression, *** ( * ( a + i ) + j )**, the variable **a** must be a 2-D array. True

(4) A char array may not end with '\0', but a string must. True

(5) In the expression,

b = ( int * ) a ;

**( int * )** represents a typecast operation. True

**[B]** Match the following pairs: [5 Marks, 1 Mark each]

| | |
|---|---|
| Shifts bits to right | >> |
| Quotient | / |
| Remainder | % |
| Check bit 1 or 0 | bitwise & |
| Post-Increment | j++ |
| Ternary operators | ? : |
| Value at address | * |
| Address of | & |
| Member access | -> |
| Unary operator | sizeof |

**[C]** Answer the following questions: [5 Marks, 1 Mark each]

(1) Create a data structure for storing the following data:

Name of document – Leaflet / Flier / Brochure
Number of colors – 1 / 2 / 4 / 5
Size – Small / Medium / Big
Type of paper – Maplitho / Bond / Artcard
Number of copies
Type of printing – Positive / Negative

```
struct doc
{
    char name[ 20 ] ;
    int numcolors ;
    int size ;
    char papertype ;
    int numcopies ;
} ;
struct doc d1, d2, d3 ;
```

(2) For storing names of months in a year, which out of array of strings and array of pointers to strings is preferable, and why?

Array of pointers to strings is preferable since it require less space and makes it easy to manipulate the strings.

(3) Consider the following structure:

```
struct Flower
{
    char name[ 20 ] ;
    int color ;
    int no_of_petals ;
} ;
struct Flower f[ 3 ] ;
```

Write statements to receive values into array **f[ ]** and print them on the screen.

```
#include <stdio.h>
#include <stdlib.h>
struct Flower
{
    char name[ 20 ] ;
    int color ;
    int no_of_petals ;
} ;
struct Flower f[ 3 ] ;
int main( )
{
    int i ;
```

```
    for ( i = 1 ; i <= 3 ; i++ )
    {
        printf( "Enter %d flower name, color and no of petals: ", i ) ;
        scanf( "%s", f[ i ].name ) ;
        scanf( "%d", &f[ i ].color ) ;
        scanf( "%d", &f[ i ].no_of_petals ) ;
    }
    for ( i = 1 ; i <= 3 ; i++ )
        printf("%s %d %d\n" ,f[i].name, f[i].color, f[i].no_of_petals) ;
    return 0 ;
}
```

(4) Given two matrices $A_{3 \times 3}$ and $B_{3 \times 3}$, define a function that checks whether matrix A is transpose of matrix B.

```
#include <stdio.h>
#define N 3
int istranspose ( int B[ ][N], int A[ ][N] ) ;
int main( )
{
    int B[ N ][ N ] = { { 1, 2, 1 }, { 2, 1, 2 }, { 1, 2, 1 } } ;
    int A[ N ][ N ] = { { 1, 2, 1 }, { 2, 1, 2 }, { 1, 2, 1 } } ;
    int flag ;
    flag = istranspose ( B, A ) ;
    if ( flag == 1 )
        printf ( "Matrix A is transpose of Matrix B\n" ) ;
    else
        printf ( "Matrix A is not a transpose of Matrix B\n" ) ;
    return 0 ;
}
int istranspose ( int B[ ][ N ], int A[ ][ N ] )
{
    int i, j, flag ;
    flag = 1 ;
    for ( i = 0 ; i < N ; i++ )
    {
        for ( j = 0 ; j < N ; j++ )
        {
            if ( B[ i ][ j ] != A[ j ][ i ] )
                return 0 ;
        }
```

```
    }
    return 1 ;
}
```

(5) What is the difference between function declaration and function definition? Which of the two—function redefinition or function redeclaration is an error, and why?

Function declaration specifies the function name, return type and parameters without the function body.

Function definition refers to the actual function that specifies the function name, return type and parameters with the function body.

Function redefinition is an error, whereas function redeclaration is not an error. This is because redeclaration is a promise that down the line the compiler would encounter a function with the given name, parameters and return type. This promise can be made any number of times. Unlike this, if the same function is defined multiple times, then during the call it will not know to which definition should control be transferred to.

(6) Write a code snippet to carry out the following operations:

Open a file 'records.dat' in read binary mode.
Skip first 200 bytes from the beginning of the file.
Read next 20 bytes into an array **arr[ ]**.

```
#include <stdio.h>
#include <stdlib.h>
int main( )
{
    FILE *fp ;
    char arr[ 25 ] ;
    fp = fopen ( "records.dat", "rb" ) ;
    {
        puts ( "Cannot open file\n" ) ;
        exit ( 1 ) ;
    }
    fseek ( fp, 200L, SEEK_SET ) ;
    fread ( arr, 20, 1, fp ) ;
```

```
    fclose( fp ) ;
    return 0 ;
}
```

(7) While using command-line arguments, is it necessary to use variables **argc** and **argv**? Write statements to print the name of the executable file and the first and second argument passed to the program?

No. Any other variables other than **argc** and **argv** can be used.

```
#include <stdio.h>
#include <stdlib.h>
int main ( int ac, char *av[ ] )
{
    printf ( "%s %s %s", av[ 0 ], av[ 1 ], av[ 2 ] ) ;
    return 0 ;
}
```

(8) Once a type has been given a new name using **typedef**, can you use the previous type? Can the effect of **typedef** be also obtained using a macro? If yes, how?

Yes, previous type can still be used as shown below:

```
typedef unsigned long int ULI ;
ULI i ;
unsigned long int j ;
```

Macros cannot be used in place of a typedef. So following program will not work.

```
#define ULI unsigned long int ;
int main( )
{
    ULI i, j, k ;
}
```

(9) What is the difference between the following declarations?

```
int *p[ 4 ] ;
```

```
int ( *q )[ 4 ] ;
```

int *p[ 4 ] - **p** is an array of 4 integer pointers.
int (* q)[ 4 ] - **q** is a pointer to an array of 4 integers.

(10) What is the difference between a structure and a union as regards:

Sharing of memory locations
Size
Accessing elements

Sharing of memory locations - Each member within a structure is assigned a unique location. As against this, elements of a union share the locations reserved for the union variable.

Size - The size of the structure is sum of sizes of its members. Size of a union is size of the longest element of the union.

Accessing elements - Individual structure members can be accessed at a time. Only one member of a union can be accessed at a time.

**[D]** Attempt the following questions: [20 Marks, 5 Marks each]

(1) Consider the following statements:

```
int a = 20 ;
int *p ;
p = &a ;
```

Write statements only using **p** to:

- set a value 45 in **a**.
- multiply **a** with 40 and store the result in **a**
- print current value of **a**

```
*p = 45;
*p = *p * 40;
printf( "%d\n", a ) ;
```

Also write statements to perform the following operations:

- Increment **p**
- After incrementation, what will be present in **p** if variable **a** is at location 4004?
- Does incrementing **p** cause a memory leak?

```
p++ ;
```

After incrementation p will contain 4008.
No incrementing p does not cause memory leak.

(2) Write a program that defines a function called **isalpha( )**. The function should receive a string and check if all characters in it are alphabets. If so, it should return a true, otherwise false. Call this function for the following strings:

"NambyPamby"
"Mumbai – 400010"

```
#include <stdio.h>
#define TRUE 1
#define FALSE 0
int isalpha ( char * ) ;
int main( )
{
    char str[ ] = "NambyPamby" ;
    int ret ;
    ret = isalpha ( str ) ;
    printf ( "%d\n", ret ) ;
}
int isalpha ( char *p )
{
    while ( *p )
    {
        if ( *p >= 'a' && *p <= 'z' || *p >= 'A' && *p <= 'Z' )
            p++ ;
        else
            return FALSE ;
    }
    return TRUE ;
}
```

(3) Define an enumeration to represent marital status of a person—single, married, divorced. Create two variables **he** and **she** of this **enum** type and assign to them values single and married respectively. Print these values and indicate what output will they produce.

```
#include <stdio.h>
#include <stdlib.h>
int main( )
{
    enum mar_status { single, married, divorced, widowed } ;
    enum mar_status he, she ;
    he = single ;
    she = married ;
    printf( "%d %d\n",he, she ) ;
    return 0 ;
}
```

Output

```
0 1
```

(4) Define functions **countzeros( )** and **countones( )** which count number of 0s and 1s in an **unsigned char** that they receive. Call both these functions for values 101 and 111. Indicate what values will these functions return?

```
#include <stdio.h>
#define _BV( x ) ( 1 << x )
unsigned char countones ( unsigned char ) ;
unsigned char countzeros ( unsigned char ) ;
int main( )
{
    int num, zeros, ones ;
    zeros = countzeros ( 101 ) ;
    ones = countones ( 101 ) ;
    printf( "0's = %d 1s = %d\n", zeros, ones ) ;
    zeros = countzeros ( 111 ) ;
    ones = countones ( 111 ) ;
    printf( "0's = %d 1s = %d\n", zeros, ones ) ;
    return 0 ;
```

```
}
unsigned char countones ( unsigned char n )
{
    int ones = 0 ;
    int i ;
    unsigned char  j, k, andmask ;
    for ( i = 7 ; i >= 0 ; i-- )
    {
        j = i ;
        andmask = _BV( j ) ;
        k = n & andmask ;
        if ( k == andmask )
            ones++ ;
    }
    return ( ones ) ;
}
unsigned char countzeros ( unsigned char n )
{
    int zeros = 0 ;
    int i ;
    unsigned char  j, k, andmask ;
    for ( i = 7 ; i >= 0 ; i-- )
    {
        j = i ;
        andmask = _BV( j ) ;
        k = n & andmask ;
        if ( k != andmask )
            zeros++ ;
    }
    return ( zeros ) ;
}
```

(5) Write a program to find maximum out of three given numbers in a single statement. What are the pros and cons of using this statement?

```
#include <stdio.h>
int main( )
{
    int a, b, c, largest ;
    printf ( "Enter three numbers: " ) ;
```

```
    scanf ( "%d %d %d", &a, &b, &c ) ;
    largest = a > b ? ( a > c ? a : c ) : ( b > c ? b : c ) ;
    printf ( "%d is the largest number.", largest ) ;
    return 0 ;
}
```

Pro - The program becomes compact
Con - Nested conditional operators are difficult to understand and debug.